WORLD POKER TOUR™

Making The
FINAL TABLE

Erick Lindgren

with Matt Matros

Collins
An Imprint of HarperCollins*Publishers*

WORLD POKER TOUR™: MAKING THE FINAL TABLE Copyright © 2005 by WPT Enterprises, Inc. All rights reserved. Printed in the United States of America. No part of this book may be used or reproduced in any manner whatsoever without written permission except in the case of brief quotations embodied in critical articles and reviews. For information address HarperCollins Publishers, 10 East 53rd Street, New York, NY 10022.

HarperCollins books may be purchased for educational, business, or sales promotional use. For information please write: Special Markets Department, HarperCollins Publishers, 10 East 53rd Street, New York, NY 10022.

The Library of Congress Cataloging-in-Publication Data has been applied for.

ISBN-10 0-06-076306–X
ISBN-13 978-0-06-076306-0

05   06   07   08   09   DIX/RRD   10   9   8   7   6   5   4   3   2   1

CONTENTS

iv

CONTENTS

PREFACE

The evolution of poker has been a remarkable thing to watch. From a business plan in 2001 to a bona fide social phenomenon in 2005, the World Poker Tour has delivered on its promise to "transform poker into a televised mainstream sports sensation." And for Lyle Berman, Robyn Moder, and everyone here at the World Poker Tour, the ride just keeps getting better.

Now trading on the NASDAQ stock exchange (symbol WPTE), WPT Enterprises is a global company broadcasting poker content in over a hundred countries worldwide. From poker chips to boxer shorts, World Poker Tour merchandise can be found in retail outlets across North America and soon around the world. At the time of publication, the next exciting phase of our business is launching with the release of www.wptonline.com—a Web site that allows users to play poker in the comfort of their own homes on the Internet.

Poker is, by its nature, a democratic sport. The World Poker Tour has always been committed to the proposition that anyone can play—and anyone can be a star. We have invited people for three years to play in our events, for two years to watch our television show, and now for nearly a year to actually own a piece of this emerging sports league—the NBA/NFL of poker. The next logical step is to extend our final table right into your home so that you can play in your pajamas.

The World Poker Tour and the phenomenon it helped launch through the powerful medium of television has changed poker forever. Giants of the game like Doyle Brunson, Jennifer Harman, and T. J. Cloutier will tell you that all poker—and particularly tournament poker—has changed dramatically with the influx of the first televised poker generation. This onslaught of charged young players has quickened the pace, increased the action, and redefined the critical art of the bluff.

Erick Lindgren represents the best that the new generation of poker players has to offer. Destined to be regarded as one of the greatest players in the game, Erick was the first player to receive the World Poker Tour "Player of the Year" award. A member of the poker brat pack, Erick constantly discusses strategy and theory with his cohorts Daniel Negreanu and Antonio Esfandiari. The result is a style that has earned the respect of players around the world.

Whether you are an accomplished poker player or new to the game, Erick's insight will help you become a winning player in the brave new world of poker. And, as the World Poker Tour expands the poker phenomenon to territories across the globe, we look forward to seeing you all at the final table.

STEVE LIPSCOMB
WPT President and Founder

FOREWORD

I still remember celebrating with Erick Lindgren on the cruise ship in Mexico. He had just beaten me at the final table of WPT's PartyPoker Million Limit Hold 'Em tournament during the second season to claim the title and $1 million prize. E-Dog ended the evening with me, along with a larger group of our friends and a few new acquaintances, by running up a $22,000 bar tab. Though I had just come in second, which always sucks, I couldn't help but be happy for my buddy and toast to his success.

I am happy to write this introduction to Erick's book because I am honored to call him a friend. He is an extremely good-natured and generous person, who's always up for anything. We have endured many of the ups and downs of living the poker life through our 20s, but we are able to keep each other grounded. Of course, we still know how to celebrate when all of the hard work pays off with a tournament win.

Daniel Negreanu, Evelyn Ng, Steve Lipscomb, and Erick at the kickoff party for the 2005 WPT World Championship

We have a lot in common. Our approach to poker is very similar, and we both learn a great deal when discussing strategy together. When not actually playing poker, we'll often make ridiculously stupid prop bets with each other. Like the last one, when we played one-on-one basketball, only he had to use his left hand and leave his right hand in his pocket! I won that one with a fluke shot at the buzzer.

E-Dog is one of the best poker players in the game today. He has an excellent approach to playing against both novice and expert players from years of playing both live and online poker.

Much of Erick's success can be attributed to frequent online play in his early 20s. While playing up to seven games at a time on three computer screens in his tiny apartment, he was able to eke out a living and begin his poker career. He learned many of his skills from those years of Internet play, in addition to conducting in-depth studies of various hands that intrigued or bothered him, and he continues this practice today. E-Dog is always willing to pass on this knowledge and has taught me a great deal about the game throughout our friendship.

As the end of WPT's second season approached, I was in the running for the WPT Player of the Year award. I needed a big finish in the championship event to overtake Erick, who'd already had two wins and a fifth-place finish in Season 2. My 41st-place finish, though, locked it up for Erick, and he won the honor of being named WPT Player of the Year. I won the award in Season 3, so now we have the proverbial rubber match in Season 4!

Now Erick has decided to share with you all some of the secrets to his success in this book. Not a bad guy to learn from, if you ask me! Whether a newcomer or a veteran player, this book will not only give you some insight into what makes the E-Dog tick, but it will also make you a better player. In his own words, he explains the kinds of actions he has taken to hone his skills over the years, the things he does to prepare for a game, and strategies that he uses to read his opponents and outplay them.

To be able to gain a solid understanding of this complicated game from a proven WPT champion is priceless. Erick, being the open and generous person that he is, has taken the pages of this book to give everyone the same high-level tips and poker strategies that have won him millions of dollars. If a tournament newbie follows E-Dog's advice, it wouldn't be a surprise to find him or her at the next WPT final table. As for me, I've got to read this book so maybe I can figure him out. Watch out, E-Dog!

DANIEL NEGREANU
World Poker Tour Player of the Year, 2004

INTRODUCTION

Two and a half years ago, poker was just another game. Then, in March of 2003, the first episode of the *World Poker Tour* aired on the Travel Channel, and a sport was created. Since then the game has exploded. WPT events have gone from 1,382 players to 7,221 players in three short seasons. Accumulated prize money has surpassed $100 million. Poker rooms across the country are expanding and busier than anyone would've thought possible a few years ago, and new poker rooms are sprouting up everywhere. The amount of money wagered daily in online cardrooms has gone from $0 in the late nineties to $179 million today, and the number of online casinos has grown exponentially. Poker has gone from a back-room game to a mainstream sport that is entertaining to watch.

If you're reading this book, chances are good that you're one of the millions of players who have been drawn into No Limit

WPT champions, Season 2: Erick Lindgren, Gus Hansen, Phil "the Unabomber" Laak, Antonio "the Magician" Esfandiari

Texas Hold 'Em by televised poker tournaments. This text aims to provide you with the strategic approach to reach a World Poker Tour (WPT) final table—a place I have been to four times and my cowriter Matt Matros has been to once. I've also been to two final tables (winning one) of the Professional Poker Tour (PPT), a brand-new tour limited to the top 200 qualifying poker players and developed by the WPT brain trust. Matt and I have combined for more than $2.7 million in winnings on the WPT/PPT. I don't tell you this to brag, but to reassure you that Matt and I have proven tournament strategies to share that will enhance your own game. Even if you've been playing this game for decades this book will will help you learn tactics to combat the opponents you're most likely to encounter at today's biggest events. These opponents include Internet qualifiers, seasoned professionals, aggressive amateurs, and converted cash-game specialists.

Any Hold 'Em player, even the newest convert to the game, will greatly benefit from reading and studying the material in this text. With that said, you should have some familiarity with No Limit Hold 'Em. In fact, these strategies are best suited for a player who has had some success in poker, but is looking to take his or her game to the next level. In addition to sharing insights and tips, *World Poker Tour: Making the Final Table* will show that there is more than one way to be a great player. We explain how Gus Hansen can win playing almost any two cards, how Phil Ivey dominates through sheer aggression, how Andy Bloch turns his opponents' aggression against them, and how all of these superstars are more than capable of changing their styles at any time.

Adjust Your Play for Success

Chapter 1 demonstrates the differences (and similarities) between cash games and tournaments and explains how you will need to adjust your play for success in the tournament environment, without *over*adjusting to the point where you pass up crucial edges. This chapter also explains why you want to be involved in satellite tournaments. The great thing about poker today is that there are ample ways to get into WPT events without paying the full entry fee. Smaller tournaments called satellites are everywhere: in cardrooms over the Internet, and in casinos/cardrooms across the country. Win a satellite, and you get the opportunity to play with the professionals in five-figure buy-in tournaments.

Understand the Risks and Rewards

It is crucial that tournament poker players have the right mind-set concerning risks and rewards before entering a major event. Chapter 2 covers the strategies and my overall philosophy for tournament poker. I believe that you must be willing to gamble with small advantages in order to be a serious contender on the tournament circuit.

Make the Most of the Early Stages

Chapters 3 and 4 explain how to make the most of the early stages of a major tournament. No Limit Hold 'Em plays drastically different when players have 100 big blinds in their stacks than it does when players have 10. You need to know how to avoid making blunders that cost all your chips, as well as how to use your large stack to build your chip count for the later stages.

Don't Let the Chip Stack Make Your Decisions

In the middle stages of a tournament, stack size becomes of paramount importance. I've made a lot of money by knowing which players become too conservative (or too desperate) with a small stack and which ones get too aggressive (or shut down too much) with a big stack. Yes, stack sizes are important, but mostly due to the fact that your opponents stray from optimal play when they let their stack sizes influence their thinking. Chapter 5 explains the tactics needed to maneuver through the middle stages of the tournament with a chip count that will give you a real chance to win the event.

Don't Get Caught Up in Bubble Thoughts

Finishing just out of the money, or "on the bubble," is one of the most frustrating things a tournament player can experience. Fortunately, for aggressive players like myself, many players approach the bubble with the sole goal of avoiding elimination at all costs. Chapter 6 shows how to take advantage of this catastrophic strategic error and explains the dramatic shift in play that happens just after the field reaches the money and all remaining players are assured of going home with some cash.

Be Mentally Prepared

The final table of a WPT televised poker tournament brings with it huge pressures and challenges unparalleled in the poker world. In Chapter 7, I will lay out how to prepare for your own final table battles, where the pride of winning and millions of dollars may be on the line.

Heads-up Takes an Additional Set of Skills

As impressive as a second-place finish in a WPT event is, it's so much sweeter, financially and psychologically, to win. I've won two of these tournaments, and I can tell you that the one-on-one, or "heads-up," portion of the event is a stage of the tournament unto itself. The difference in first- and second-place prize money is so great that I devote all of Chapter 8 to heads-up tactics. I hope they will pay off for you in a big way.

The World Poker Tour has become huge, with a continually growing television audience and number of entrants—some fields more than seven times as large in Season 3 as they were in Season 1. It's only going to get bigger. Don't miss *your* chance to cash in on this unique era in poker history. I wish you success, patience, and a lot of luck in your poker future.

CHAPTER ONE

Welcome to the World Poker Tour

Growing up, I never thought I would be on TV. Sure, I dreamed about making it as a quarterback, or a hoopster, or even (dare I say it) as a politician. But I never figured there was any realistic chance that Erick Lindgren would become a name anyone other than my family and friends recognized. I'm a small-town guy, from the 3,000-person hamlet of Burney, California, in the Sierra Nevadas, and I thought I'd always be a small-town guy. Now I live in Las Vegas.

Poker, and more specifically the World Poker Tour (WPT), is responsible for this transformation. I didn't see that one coming

2

either. There weren't poker tournaments of any kind anywhere near my hometown, let alone televised poker tournaments. When I went off to nearby Butte Junior College in California to start my education, I didn't know I would be only miles away from the Colusa Indian Casino. Unfortunately, I never got my degree. In my second year I dropped out, and by the time I was 21 I was playing poker professionally. I won my first major tournament, the Bellagio Five Diamond Poker Classic in Las Vegas,

Nevada, at age 26. Since then I've won two World Poker Tour events, one Professional Poker Tour event, and made two other World Poker Tour final tables.

That was my road to the WPT. Yours will be easier. These days, anyone can get all the experience he or she needs no matter how far from a cardroom he lives. Players can improve at a much faster rate than has ever been possible thanks to the wealth of information available, and the easy access of online poker rooms. Even if online poker is not your thing, there are innumerable ways for the small-time player to enter big-time tournaments without paying the full entry fee, which will often be $10,000 or more. Believe it or not, it's easy to get to the World Poker Tour. I'll show you not just how to get there, but how to win there.

The beauty of poker is that within a few minutes anybody can understand the basics. After perhaps one semi-uncomfortable night, any poker neophyte can become one of the guys or girls that has a chance to win a tournament. Almost anyone can win. This is what separates our game from so many others. Not only does the best player sometimes lose, but he or she can be defeated by the most amateur of amateurs. This fact convinces many poor players to invest in poker tournaments. Anyone can win, so why not them? Testosterone-filled men think they can bully their way to the title, and cagey, savvy, intelligent players from both sexes are drawn to the game, assuming they can outwit their opposition to victory. Poker sounds easy, but the secret is, it's not. The old adage that it takes a minute to learn and a lifetime to master is definitely true. There are actually very few obstacles to becoming a top player, but the trick is to know what those obstacles are. I will show you. This book will provide a strategic guideline to No Limit Hold 'Em and give examples of how I and many of the top pros think. The hard work, however, is up to you. Feel free to remain a recreational winner or a lovable loser, but if you study this book and play lots and lots of poker, then maybe I will see you at a final table.

Are You Ready for the Next Level?

Since you've picked up this book, I'm going to assume you know how to play a little poker. You know how Texas Hold 'Em works, and you're probably good enough to make some money off your friends in your home game, or the low- to mid-limit games at your local casino. If this is not the case, and you are just learning the game, you might want to pick up one or two beginner's poker books before tackling this one. I suggest *World Poker Tour: Shuffle Up and Deal,* by Mike Sexton, or *The Making of a Poker Player,* by my coauthor Matt Matros.

If you're not a rank beginner, but all your poker experience has been playing Limit Hold 'Em, let me briefly go over the key differences between Limit and No Limit Hold 'Em (because in case you haven't figured it out, this book is a strategy guide to *No Limit* Hold 'Em). In No Limit, the minimum bet is always equal to the big blind, and the maximum bet is always as much money as you have on the table. In $10–$20 Limit Hold 'Em, a game with $5 and $10 blinds, you have to bet $20 if you want to bet on the turn. In a $5–$10 blind No Limit Hold 'Em game, you can bet $10 or $10,000 on the turn (assuming you have $10,000 in front of you). The other major difference between the two games is that No Limit Hold 'Em sometimes requires all players to ante, especially late in tournaments. This makes the pot much bigger in relation to the blinds, and usually creates a lot of action.

OK, so either you've read a book or two and feel confident, or you've proven to yourself through your results that you're a winning cash-game player. You're probably very patient. You probably know that you can fold every hand for hours and hours if you have to, and still have a winning session if you drag that monster pot you've been waiting for all night. You're good. You can make money at this game. And now you want to try a tournament. Maybe you find the adrenaline rush bigger in tournaments. Maybe you're a former athlete like me and are trying to bring competition back into your life. Maybe you just want to prove to yourself that you're as good as the best players in the world. If any of these justifications resonate with you, then I think you've made a good decision. Give tournament poker a try.

Tournaments vs. Cash Games

First, know that in poker tournaments you don't have the luxury of patience. The blinds continually rise, and if you try to fold your way through a run of bad cards you'll find yourself on the rail. It's not that tournaments necessitate a different strategy from ring games, it's just that when the blinds and antes are very large in relation to your stack, it becomes correct to play a lot more hands, and to play them very aggressively. In No Limit Hold 'Em cash games, the blinds are very small in relation to your stack and there is less reason for players to get involved.

For example, let's say you're dealt K-2o (o = offsuit) on the button in two different No Limit Hold 'Em scenarios. In both scenarios, you have 10,000 chips and everyone folds to you. In Scenario One, the blinds are $10 and $20. In Scenario Two, the blinds are $1,000 and $2,000 and everyone has anted $200. You should almost certainly fold in Scenario One. The reward from stealing the blinds is very small; if you get reraised you have to fold, and if you get called you have a hand that is very difficult to play after the flop and beyond. In Scenario Two, you should almost certainly raise all-in. If you steal the blinds and antes you increase your stack by 50 percent. You can't get reraised, and if you get called you don't have to worry about playing your hand after the flop. Although you'll probably only win about 30 percent of the time when you get called, that's more than enough to make moving in correct if the blinds will fold to the all-in as little as one-third of the time. We'll go over the math of these all-in situations in more detail later, but for now you should understand that the size of the blinds and antes wildly impacts the decisions we make at the table. Notice that I didn't specify whether each scenario was from a cash game or a tournament. I wanted to make the point that the essential difference between cash games and tournament play is the size of the blinds. If you are a ring-game player looking to take on tournament poker, try hosting a home game in which a player can only buy in for 10 big blinds at a time. Then, if several players have had to take a few rebuys, double the blinds. If the blinds are constantly threatening to eat away players' stacks, you'll have successfully simulated a tournament atmosphere.

The other option for tournament immersion is to start entering low-stakes tournaments, which these days are plentiful. If you play Internet poker, you can find dozens of tournaments with buy-ins of $10 or less every day.

The big secret about tournament poker is that it's not all that different from the normal cash-game poker you'll see spread 24-hours-a-day in cardrooms all over the world. If you play your basic winning cash-game strategy, you should be able to make some money in the small tournaments. I'll discuss this in detail next chapter, but don't be afraid to jump into a tournament even if you've never played one. Tournament skills are not nearly as specialized as most players think. How else do you explain Howard Lederer, Barry Greenstein, and Chau Giang, all long-time professional cash-game players, tearing up the World Poker Tour over the course of its first three seasons?

OK, so you've played 10 or 20 low-stakes tournaments and you're starting to feel comfortable. Maybe you've made a final table or two. Heck, maybe you've even won one. Should you jump into a World Poker Tour event? Well, no, but you might still be able to play one. Every WPT venue also hosts satellite tournaments, smaller events whose top prizes are seats into the big WPT tournament. Foxwoods Resort Casino in Connecticut has a particularly ingenious system for this. For $60, Foxwoods likes to say, you too can play a WPT event, win millions of dollars, and appear on TV. How? By entering a $60 one-table tournament, which Foxwoods calls Act One, advancing to a $150 one-table tournament (Act Two), advancing into a $1,050 multitable tournament (Act Three), and then winning a seat in the $10,000 buy-in World Poker Finals championship. I highly recommend that new tournament players enter whatever satellites they can to try to play a big event. Be aware, however, that the most likely result of putting up $60 to try to enter the World Poker Finals is a loss of $60. These satellites are not fantastic moneymaking opportunities for inexperienced players, in the short term. But they provide invaluable lessons if you're fortunate enough to win a seat in a main event, and go toe-to-toe with the best poker players in the world.

Entering a Set Elite

I won my seat in the 2003 Ultimate Poker Classic by winning a satellite online. That event ended up being my first win on the WPT. My cowriter, Matt Matros, played three World Poker Tour events by winning satellites into them. He didn't make any money on his first three, but then in April of 2004 he satellited into the World Poker Tour $25,000 buy-in championship event, finished third, and won $706,903. Playing satellites may not pay off immediately, but it is a great long-term investment for the experience alone. Let's look at some of the strategies you'll need to navigate your way through the satellites and find yourself in a WPT tournament.

First, we must distinguish between a one-table satellite and a super satellite. In a one-table satellite, there is typically only one winner, and that winner gets a seat into the main event. New players will probably not want to take on a one-table satellite, since even a one-table satellite for a main event will usually cost more than a thousand dollars! Much more accessible to the inexperienced player are the super satellites. In these tournaments, hundreds of players may enter for a few hundred dollars each, and there will be as many seats into the big tournament awarded as the prize pool will allow. For example, if 200 people put up 200 dollars each in a super satellite for a $10,000 event, there will be $40,000 in the prize pool and the top four finishers will get seats. In these events, play at the final table is drastically different from the play of a one-table satellite. In a one-table satellite, the winner-take-all prize structure means that you have to do everything you can to get all the chips at the table. Folding often in an attempt to get to the final two or three is a sure way to spend a long time in one-table satellites and almost never make any money. Compare that to a super satellite giving four seats. First place equals fourth place! In this pay structure, it is clearly correct in the endgame to sit on the sidelines and watch as many people bust as you can. I am not particularly fond of super satellites for this reason, as I am an aggressive player who likes to try to win chips. Nevertheless, I am smart enough to understand why constant aggression is not the best approach in a super satellite, and that understanding has won me a lot of seats.

Before you start worrying about super satellite final table strategy, you first have to get to the final table. To give a new player his best chance to do that, I'm going to describe some of the common characteristics of a super satellite.

1. Players are given very few chips relative to the blinds to start. Super satellites are designed to be over in a few hours, five at most. Some start players with just $200 in chips and rapidly increase the blinds. In these events, you can't wait around for big pairs. You've got to be aggressive with marginal holdings.

2. Players have the chance to rebuy. Many super satellites have unlimited rebuys—options for players to buy more chips when they have the amount they started with or less—for the first hour (which is the main method by which money gets into the prize pool). It is important to know whether you should rebuy, so you don't spend time thinking about it when you should be thinking about playing poker.

Value of Chips and Knowing When to Rebuy

At the beginning of tournaments, chips are worth more to good players than they are to bad players. This is because the tournament is worth more to good players than bad players. Bad players lose money; good players win money. That's how the poker world works. So if a good player buys in for $200 and gets 200 tournament chips, they might be worth $300 in real money. Whereas if a bad player buys in for $200 and gets 200 tournament chips, those same chips might only be worth $100 to him in real money. Early in a tournament, each additional chip added to your stack is worth pretty much the same as the chips already in your stack. So if a good player rebuys for another $200, the 400 chips he now has in his stack are probably worth somewhere close to $600—say $590. Eventually, even a good player sees a diminishing return, because obtaining more chips isn't as important for a huge stack, especially in a super satellite. But this effect is probably only noteworthy if the new chips increase the player's stack size by a small amount.

The point of all this is that, for a good player, it often makes sense to rebuy. The rule of thumb is the bigger the seat you're trying to win, the more correct it is to rebuy. This is also true for add-ons, an additional purchase of chips usually allowed after the rebuy period has ended. Say you have an average stack of 1,000 chips after the rebuy period with 40 players left in a super satellite giving out two seats. Since you're a good player, you figure you have about a 10 percent chance to win a seat with those thousand chips. You're trying to decide whether to add on 400 chips for $400, which would probably increase your chances of winning a seat to about 16 percent. If you're trying to win a seat for a $4,000 tournament, you shouldn't take the add-on. Your chips are worth $400, and adding on does not double their value. But if you're trying to win a seat for a $10,000 tournament, you should definitely add on. Spending the $400 increases your equity by $600—a $200 gain.

Whatever decisions you make concerning rebuys or add-ons, try not to let the money influence you. Some players will buy in to a tournament for $200 and then refuse to take any rebuys or add-ons even when it's obviously correct to do so. They don't want to triple or quadruple their original investment. This mind-set will kill you. If you're playing a rebuy tournament, you shouldn't be afraid to rebuy many times if that's the right thing to do. If three or four rebuys represent a significant fraction of your bankroll, then you should find a smaller tournament to play in. You should decide beforehand how many rebuys you are willing to stomach, and then make your decisions about whether to use them based on what you think is correct, not based on how much money you've already invested. Matt once put $1,400 into a super satellite for a $10,000 buy-in event, which might have been more than anyone else in the field. But he was also one of only three people to win a seat.

3. Players gamble early. This is especially true if there is a rebuy period. Players are often willing to go all-in with any ace or even any two suited cards if they know they can just rebuy when they run out of chips. If this happens at your table, you've got to be willing to gamble with the maniacs. Normally marginal hands like A-10 and 7-7 become monsters if your opponent is capable of holding A-2, 3-3, 9-4s (s = suited), or worse. Of course, the more you get involved, the more bad beats you'll take and the more likely you yourself will have to rebuy. That comes with the territory. It's a small price to pay for getting your chips in the pot with fantastic prospects of doubling or tripling up and putting yourself in prime position to win a seat before the rebuy period even ends.

4. Endgame strategy is completely different from normal tournaments. As I mentioned earlier, play is a lot different when fourth place equals first place. Let's look at some specific adjustments you'll have to make.

In a typical tournament, you should usually be trying to get more and more chips until you have the tournament won. In a super satellite, when you've reached two-thirds of the final average stack size, you should probably stop taking risks to get chips. Here's an example. There are 120,000 chips in play in a super satellite (by the way, you should always find out how many chips are in whatever tournament you're playing) and you have 5,000. They are giving out four seats. So you know that when all is said and done, the average stack size of the final four players will be 30,000. In a normal tournament, you'd want to position yourself so that you'd have above-average chips when it got four-handed, giving yourself a good chance to win the whole thing. In a super satellite, you don't need to win the whole thing. In this case, you only need to come in fourth, and having one chip remaining in your stack when there are four players left is as good as having 119,000. I'm suggesting that once you reach 20,000 chips, you don't need any more. This is because there are usually short stacks trying to sneak into the final seat during the endgame. Having two-thirds of the final average stack should give you an excellent chance to win your seat.

Attack the Blinds

Remember, however, that this is poker. Once you hit 20,000 chips in this example, you need to hold on to them, and you can't do that by folding every hand. The blinds and antes will eat your stack away, and soon you'll be the one praying you can fold your way into a seat. That's not a reliable method for winning (although Matt once won a seat in a super satellite ending up with fewer chips than he started with!). To maintain your stack, you need to keep attacking the blinds of tight players, and you need to protect your premium hands from getting beaten by making large raises with them. You do not need to call a raise for a significant portion of your chips without a monster hand. You're trying to tread water and avoid busting, you're not trying to increase your stack. You'll see in the next chapter, and indeed throughout the rest of the book, that this philosophy is exactly the opposite of the one I recommend for real tournaments. But at the end of super satellites, survival trumps chip gathering. This is why there is a breed of players who excel at super satellites by playing survival poker, but are unable to make a score in a real tournament. The skill sets for the two endgames are almost diametrically opposed.

When you're lucky enough to reach "the bubble," when only one player needs to bust before everyone remaining gets a seat, play again is drastically different from any other kind of poker. First, you need to figure out who is going to be the first player blinded out. Sometimes this is the player with the shortest stack, but not always. Because the blinds are so big and players are clinging to their chips, there is sometimes more than one player who can't make it through a round of blinds and antes. In these cases, it's all a matter of who has to post his blinds first. If the next player to be blinded out is you, you need to take action. Move all-in with anything remotely reasonable and hope either everyone folds or you double up. If you don't move in, the other players will just wait you out. No one else is likely to go broke, even with a big hand, before you have to post your blinds. The notable exception to this is if there are two or more clueless players remaining who think they're supposed to try to come in first. If that's happening, you should fold almost every hand, praying one of them busts the other.

If you're not the next to bust, you want to make sure the

person who is never gets a free pass. You should raise his blind liberally, but only if you have the chips to do it. If you will be the second person blinded out, you are pretty much forced to play a waiting game—as in, wait to see if the other guy busts before making a move yourself. That said, you still have to play if you get dealt a premium hand. Let's say you have enough chips to go one orbit, but there is a player who will be all-in on the big blind next hand. That player folds, and so does everyone else, and you look down at A-A on the button. The blinds have a lot of chips. Should you play? Well, the chances of your aces holding up against one caller are about 85 percent, and the chance that you'll get called at all is probably 30 percent or less. So you're only looking at about a 5 percent chance of busting, should you move in. You should probably also move in with kings or queens. Anything else and things start to get dicey. That's the thing about super satellite final tables—they're not about getting the most chips, they're about finding a way to eliminate the short stacks.

Let's look at a few hypothetical hands from super satellite final tables. In all cases, there are five players left, and four seats are being awarded.

Q: You have the second fewest chips, but you will bust first because the shortest stack just got through his blinds and he is the button. UTG (under the gun; the first player to act after the hand is dealt) folds, and you look down at K-9o. What is your play?

A: You should move all-in. K-9o is significantly better than a random hand, and you should want to take this hand up against the big blind rather than wait for a random hand in the big blind yourself. You can't count on someone busting in the next two hands. You have to try to get some chips.

Q: You have the second-fewest chips, only enough for one orbit, but the short stack is UTG and will post all-in on his big blind next hand. He folds, and you look down at K-9o. What is your play?

A: Fold. The risk of busting if you take K-9o against the big blind is far too great here, since folding gives you about a 70 percent chance of winning a seat on the next hand alone.

Q: You are the big stack, and the other four players have fewer than 2 orbits of chips in front of them. Two of them have fewer than 1 orbit. You have 15 orbits of chips. You are dealt A-A UTG. What is your play?

A: You probably shouldn't even know that you have A-A, because you're wasting everyone's time by looking at your hand. There is no reason to play anything here, including A-A. Fold. The chance of all four players accumulating chips and one of them busting you is less than 1 percent. This chance only goes up if you enter the pot voluntarily.

The Big Day

Now that you're super satellite savvy, I'm confident you'll put this knowledge to use and win your way into a World Poker Tour event. Let me tell you what to expect once you get there.

First, you'll have a lot of chips at the beginning. A typical $100 tournament starts its players with stacks of 75 big blinds or so. To my knowledge, no World Poker Tour event starts its players with fewer than 200 big blinds. The WPT Championship starts its players with $50,000 in chips and blinds of only $50 and

$100—the biggest starting stack in any tournament as of this writing. Having a lot of chips means fewer hands are worth playing for an all-in raise. We'll get into this in much more detail in chapter 3.

The levels will be long. Whereas most tournaments increase the blinds every half hour or less, WPT events increase the blinds between 60 and 90 minutes with the Final Table at 60 minutes. Not only that, a WPT tournament takes four or five days or more to finish. If you're not used to focusing for long stretches of time, or if you've never played a tournament that lasts more than a day, I would strongly recommend you strengthen your stamina before the big event. If you work out regularly, great. You probably don't need to add anything to your regimen. To my readers who don't work out, you should at least go for a couple of jogs in the weeks leading up to the tournament. If you're against any form of physical conditioning whatsoever, some players practice meditation as a means to train themselves to stay focused at the table. I personally believe there is no substitute for staying in shape, but do whatever works for you to keep you alert at the felt.

Finally, and most important, the quality of play will be better in a WPT event than what you're used to seeing in small buy-in tournaments. A lot of beginning players have a strategy that will earn them money against the typical foes you'd come across in a $50 tournament. These strategies often include making big laydowns, never calling reraises without premium hands, playing very tight early only, and milking opponents by slow-playing nut hands. While there is a time and place for each of these tactics, most of them will be ineffective against professionals (although they might still work against some of the weak players who have won their way into the tournament via satellite!). It's great that you have a strategy to beat the low-stakes players, but on the World Poker Tour, you're going to need a strategy that stands a chance against the likes of John Juanda, Barry Green-stein, Howard Lederer, Daniel Negreanu, Gus Hansen, Phil Ivey, and, of course, me.

Throughout the rest of this book, I'm going to give you all the information you need to get to a WPT final table, and to succeed once there. I'll give you the mind-set, the philosophy, the tactics and strategy, and even the plays that have gotten me to four WPT final tables. I want everyone to experience for themselves the euphoria that poker has been gracious enough to give me.

CHAPTER TWO

Winning Tournament Philosophy

There is a gross misconception among so many poker players about how tournaments should be approached, about what a player's overall goal in a tournament should be, and what the best strategy is for winning money in poker tournaments. Many players believe the goal in a poker tournament is to survive as long as possible—to cling to one's chips as long as one can while watching everyone else go broke. You'll hear these players say things like "You can't win the tournament in the first hour, but you sure can lose it," or "I don't like to get my chips in when my best case is only a 6-to-5 favorite," or "Before you win, you have to make it to the final table."

Poker Is Not About Survival

Players are so misguided about what they're actually supposed to be doing when they enter a poker tournament that I'm
devoting an entire chapter to the philosophy of tournament
poker. I want you to have the correct mind-set going in to any
event you enter. It's the mind-set shared by nearly all top players,
including Daniel Negreanu, Gus Hansen, Phil Ivey, Barry Greenstein, me and pretty much anyone else you can think of. And here
it is in one sentence: *tournament poker is not about survival; tournament poker is about accumulating chips.*

I understand if you don't accept that statement immediately. After all, it's counterintuitive. The guy or girl that survives the longest wins the poker tournament—so why isn't a poker tournament about survival? I'll explain. Poker is a game of risk and reward. If you're a winning cash-game player, you know, for example, that bad beats are part of what makes the game profitable in the long run. If the best hand held up every time, no one would ever chase long-shot draws in the hopes of getting lucky. Most of the time, chasers won't get lucky, and the solid player who had the best hand from the beginning will drag the chips. This concept extends to tournaments.

If you play tournaments with survival as your goal, you'll be less likely to be eliminated on any given hand than a player who is playing correctly. You'll be less likely to take a bad beat than a player who is playing correctly. But just as absorbing bad beats is a necessary part of winning cash-game play, engaging with your opponents at the risk of losing chips is a necessary part of winning tournament play. A player's chance of winning a tournament at any given time is equal to the percentage of total chips he has (assuming players are of equal skill). If you play to survive, you're going to have a hard time accumulating chips along the way. Think about it from a risk/reward perspective. The reward for playing survival poker is to cash in the tournament far more often than the average player, say 25 percent of the time versus 10 percent of the time, with only a small chance of winning the tournament—say half the chance of the average player who cashes, and that's being very generous. The reward for playing with chip accumulation as your goal is that you'll win the tournament 2 to 2.5 times as often as the average player. The risk is that you'll often bust early, probably only cashing as often as an average player. So doing the math, the Chip Gatherer will win the tournament between 1.6 and 2 times as often as the Survivor, but the Survivor will cash 2.5 times as often as the Chip Gatherer. Now, for our last step, let's look at typical prize structures. First place usually gets 30 to 40 percent of the prize pool. The first player who cashes usually gets his buy-in back. It's pretty clear that the Chip Gatherer will win far more money than the Survivor in the long run.

Expected Value

You'll hear players talk all the time about how they don't want to "risk their entire tournament on one hand." Good players hope they get the chance to risk their entire tournament on several consecutive hands, because that means they've found positive expected value (EV) situations on which to risk their chips.

EV is the amount of money a poker situation is worth in the long run. For example, if you get two aces as the first player to act (under the gun, or UTG) in No Limit Hold 'Em, that situation might have an EV of 10 big blinds. There might be times when you lose 100 big blinds, and times when you win 200 big blinds, but if you played 1,000 hands you would *expect* to be ahead 10,000 big blinds. That's 10 big blinds per hand, meaning your EV is 10. Of course, I'm just making up this number. The actual EV of holding A-A UTG in No Limit Hold 'Em depends on who your opponents are, how many chips everyone has, and how well you play. The point is, as thinking players, we can confidently say that playing aces is a plus-EV play—a play that is "getting the best of it." And that's what matters. In a cash game, the pertinent question always is "What decision should I make so that I earn the most chips in the long run?"

The truth is that this is almost always the pertinent question in tournaments as well. The more chips you have, the better chance you have to win the tournament. Look at the prize structure and you'll see that maximizing your chance to win almost always maximizes the amount of real money you'll expect to make. There are exceptions, and I will get into those exceptions over the course of the book. Most of them occur at the final table, when folding in a marginal situation can mean instantly earning a few hundred thousand dollars by moving up a spot. But the exceptions are just that—exceptions. The rule is, do everything you can to win the tournament.

Problems with Waiting for a Bad Player to Bust

The common refrain that serves as a counterargument to what I've just written goes something like this: "I'm a good enough player so that I don't have to put my chips in with only a marginal edge. I'll find a better spot to get my chips in later. And if I'm going to risk my entire tournament on one hand, I want to be confident I have the best hand. By playing this way, I can wait for all the bad players to bust, make sure I get into the money, and *then* worry about trying to win the tournament."

There are many, many problems with this line of thinking. I'll try to enumerate them.

1. Most players are not as good as they think they are.

The way we make money in poker is by finding positive-EV situations. If you think you're such a good player that you can knowingly pass up a positive-EV situation, all I can say is you'd better be right. It's not as though we get a lot of positive-EV situations over the course of a poker tournament. Most hands we get dealt junk and have to fold preflop. If you pass up a positive-EV play, who's to say you'll ever get another one? There's no Law of Poker Justice that says, "If thou makest a tight fold, thou shalt be rewarded with pocket kings." In fact, at any given point in a tournament, there is a reasonable chance you'll go hours without seeing a playable hand. So unless you're an absolute master at turning garbage hands into gold, you'd better think long and hard before passing up a chance to get your chips in with the best of it.

2. Most "marginal" edges are not as marginal as people think. Let's look at a quick example from a WPT final table. During the L.A. Poker Classic in Season Two, Vinny Vinh opened the pot with K-9s. Mike Keohan, an amateur player, elected to reraise with A-Q. I thought this was a good decision on Mike's part. He had a powerful hand for the situation, especially since there were only four players at the table. But here's where things got dicey. Vinny Vinh, in studying Keohan, must have sensed some weakness because he decided to reraise all-in. A shocked Mike Keohan thought for a little while and folded his hand. Presumably, Mike's reasons for folding were that he didn't want to risk busting out of the tournament and that his opponent might have had A-K or a big pair. What you have to understand is that Mike was being offered about 2-to-1 pot odds on his money. Even if Vinny could've *only* had pocket eights or better, or A-K, Mike still would've been positive-EV (in terms of chips) to call. And that's the absolute worst case. As it turned out, Keohan's call, if he had made it, would've been worth about 600,000 in chip EV. Six hundred thousand chips. Now I ask you, is that a marginal edge?

3. There is very little value in remaining in the tournament. People don't want to risk "their whole tournament." But the value of "their whole tournament" is, at least early on, equal to the amount of chips in their stack. There is no value in still being alive in the tournament. If you're in a $10,000 buy-in WPT event and you've got $20,000 in starting chips, then your tournament—your "whole" tournament—is worth $10,000. If three hours later you're still in and you still have $20,000, then your "whole" tournament is still worth $10,000. There is almost no value in staying in the tournament without accumulating chips. So why wouldn't you risk chips if it's the correct thing to do, if by risking "your whole tournament" you actually increase the value of "your whole tournament"?

4. You don't need the best hand to be plus-EV. I often see players post two-thirds of their stack in the big blind and then fold to an all-in raise from the button, showing 2-4o, or 9-3o, or some other trash hand and saying, "I'm pretty sure he could beat that." These players are missing the point. There is no particular reason you have to have the best hand when putting your chips in. What you do have to have is positive EV. If you've posted half your stack on the big blind, and all players have folded to the button, the player on the button is going to raise your blind with a lot of hands. But more important, after the small blind folds, you'll be getting 3.5-to-1 pot odds to call. That means you only need to win 22 percent of the time to make the call plus-EV. Against the button's range, any two cards you might hold will win at least that often. Players who make this fold will survive longer than they should—and they'll be throwing away money.

5. Getting "in the money" is not the goal. As I've already discussed, you need to give yourself a chance to win the tournament. If your goal is simply to cash and earn a profit, you will find yourself cashing far more often than an average player—but you will almost never win the event. Everyone loves to tell stories about the time they came back from having just one chip to win the tournament. Despite these tales, waiting for the nuts when you're short-stacked because you've seen people win from that spot before is not the appropriate strategy. The appropriate strategy is to press every edge, which usually means getting your short stack into the pot as fast as possible. That's how you build up chips to fight with. That's how you get into the money *with a stack*. And that's how you win tournaments.

Playing Aggressive Poker

OK, I've spent a lot of time now discussing tournament philosophy in the abstract. Let's take a look at some real-world, practical applications of playing aggressive poker the way I suggest.

Hand One: Blinds are $200–$400 and you have $15,000 in chips. It's folded to you in the cutoff and you look down at A-Ko. You raise to $1,100 and the button immediately reraises to $3,000. The blinds fold. What's your play?

Answer: You move all-in. A-Ko is a powerful hand in No Limit Hold 'Em, and the button could easily be making a move on you, thinking you were raising based on the strength of your position and not the strength of your cards. Some players call "to look at a flop" in this situation. While that might be OK once in a while as a way to vary your game, it should not be your typical play here. A-K is only a small underdog to medium pairs, but that's if the hand goes to the river. A-K has about a 1-in-3 chance to flop a pair—so if you just call to look at a flop, two-thirds of the time you'll be giving up on the flop. Not only that, the times when you hit the flop the middle pair probably won't pay you. I mean, would *you* pay off a guy if you have two sevens when the flop comes ace-high? We want to give the middle pair a chance to fold. We don't want to give him more information and let him look at a flop before making that decision. So we put him to a choice pre-flop. A-K is only in real trouble against pocket aces or pocket kings. Since we have one of each of those cards in our hand, it is only half as likely that our opponent has a huge pocket pair.

By deciding to call the reraise, or to fold to the reraise in an effort to "preserve your chips" or "not risk your entire tournament on a drawing hand" (other phrases I hear all the time), you are typically costing yourself a lot of money. Play to accumulate chips, not to survive.

Hand Two: There are 35 players left in a World Poker Tour event. Twenty-seventh place gets $25,000 while 28th place gets a pat on the back and a "better luck next time." You have pocket 10s, put in a standard raise, and get one caller. The flop comes nine-high with two hearts and you decide to check, hoping for a check-raise. Your opponent obliges and bets. You check-raise, putting in about a third of your stack. Your opponent instantly and vocally declares that he's all-in. And he has you covered. You've been playing with this guy all day, and you are very confident that he has only a flush draw. He moved his chips in with emphasis, and loudly announced his all-in, and every other time he's done so he's been on a semi-bluff. What's your play?

Answer: You call. While it's very tempting to fold and try your best to secure 27th place, the ultimate goal is first. First is your ultimate goal not just because it helps the ego, but because that's where the money is. You've already committed a healthy chunk of your stack to this pot. That fact, plus your confident read of your opponent, makes this call just about automatic. If you won't be capable of making calls like this at bubble time, you shouldn't be entering WPT events in the first place.

Hand Three: You're Russell Rosenblum at the final table of the 2004 WPT Championship. Richard Grijalva, a young, aggressive player and one of the chip leaders at the table, opens for a raise. You have A-Qo and decide to reraise, putting in about half your chips. It folds around to Richard, who moves all-in. There are five players left, and you were fifth in chips before the hand started. What's your play?

Answer: As should be clear from the L.A. Poker Classic hand I analyzed earlier, when you're getting 3 to 1 on your money against an aggressive player, you have to call with ace-queen. You've committed yourself. Russell took some criticism for committing himself with ace-queen in this situation. To me, this criticism is ludicrous. He was facing an aggressive player who was capable of opening the pot with a wide range of hands, and Russell had the fewest chips at the table. There was nothing to be gained by sitting around waiting for a better hand than ace-queen. Ace-queen has an unfounded reputation as a bad hand in No Limit Hold 'Em. Sure you would fold ace-queen to an early position raise, or to a raise and a reraise—but against a possible steal-raise, or steal-reraise, ace-queen is a monster. In the actual hand, Russell called, Richard had pocket jacks, Russell didn't improve and he was eliminated. It's better to be eliminated playing well than it is to remain in the tournament playing poorly. Really, it is!

Hand Four: It is the first hand of the tournament. You have $10,000 in chips and the blinds are $25 and $50. It's folded to you in middle position and you look down at two aces. You raise to $150. The next three players fold, but the small blind then moves all-in for $10,000! The big blind folds. What's your play?

Answer: Honest to goodness, I hear players advocate folding here all the time. If you've read everything I've written up to this point, your answer better be that you call instantly and delightedly. If it even crossed your mind that folding and ensuring survival in the tournament might be the best play, please go back to the beginning of the chapter and read it all again!

The Only Goal Is Winning

Make no mistake about it, the class of players who look to fold and survive are one of the biggest reasons I've won two World Poker Tour events. When I enter a poker tournament, my goal—my *only* goal—is to win it. If you don't know whether you're a player capable of winning the tournament, your goal should still be to win it. To improve as a player, it is helpful to accept that this is a game of luck. None of us can change that. The skill in this game is not in avoiding risk, it is in taking the correct risks. The last three winners of the WPT World Championship—Martin de Knijff, Alan Goehring, and Tuan Le—were unafraid to get their chips in the pot. In fact, I can't think of a single winner on the World Poker Tour who played "to survive." You want to be a great poker player? Stop thinking you're better than the randomness of the game. Embrace the randomness. Let people think you're a wild risk taker. And start taking advantage of those afraid to risk their own chips.

Chapter Three

The Tournament Starts

So you've made it. Either you have won a super satellite or have become confident enough in your abilities and your bankroll to buy in directly to the event. But one way or another, you have found yourself in a televised, five-figure buy-in event on the World Poker Tour. Congratulations, you are in for an adrenaline-pumping day you're likely to remember for the rest of your life.

The first thing to do is catch your breath and understand that you're in for a long day. Most WPT events feature a 10-to-12-hour Day One, if you're lucky enough to make it that far. Your

Erick contemplating his next move against Daniel Negreanu at the PPT.

focus in hour 12 needs to be just as sharp as, if not sharper than, your focus in hour one. Do whatever you need to do to make this happen. Get plenty of sleep. Eat breakfast. Go for a morning jog. Anything you can do to help your stamina will increase your edge in the tournament.

Know Your Opponents

OK, you've done the preparation and you're ready to play all afternoon and into the night. You get your seat assignment and you approach the table. Let's pretend you are me. The first thing I do when I get to the table is assess the opposition. I spot the players I know and I try to judge how they are feeling right at this moment. Do they look tired? Have they shaved? Are they wearing the same clothes they wore the night before? I'm looking for any information I can get. Should I pick on this person early or is he a strong player I will try to avoid? This is the question I am striving to answer. One of the keys, and perhaps *the* key, to winning tournaments is to play pots with the weaker players and avoid the top pros unless you have position. Even then tread lightly. Fear no player, but know where your edge comes from. Your edge comes from the people in over their heads.

Look for Weakness

After I've assessed the players I know, I move to the weaker players. I assume each player I don't know is weak until he or she proves otherwise. But there are different kinds of weakness. There is the weak player who will raise every hand, the weak player who will fold every hand, the weak player who will check-call far too often, and the weak player who will try to raise me just because he wants to say he made a move on a known pro. If you're not a known pro, there might be players who want to raise you just for *that* reason. The point is, you have to know what you're up against, and you can start gathering that information before the first hand is dealt.

Let's say I have drawn seat four at our nine-handed table. Seat one is a young player I haven't seen before. Let's look further. He has spent a lot on his wardrobe and has stylish, expensive sunglasses. His shirt is untucked and he handles his chips like a veteran, riffling them without effort. My read: this guy is going to be aggressive. Now, I'm not saying all players with these characteristics are aggressive, I'm saying that in poker we take every advantage we can get. The fact is that 90 percent of the time or more I will be right in my assessment of this player in the one seat. The read was really somewhat obvious, and actually, the read was the easy part. The hard part is knowing how to take advantage of such a player.

Be Careful of Aggressive Players

Aggressive players are the least predictable. Since an aggressive style is usually a strong style, I'm not too inclined to immediately engage my aggressive opponents. In the case of the one seat, I'm not looking to battle with him right away. Instead, I'll let him show his style of play first while I continue to build my opinion of him.

In seat two we have an older, but not ancient, gentleman. He has a clean collared shirt, but it is far from a designer brand. His hair is groomed carefully and his shirt is tucked perfectly in his slacks. This person is probably a very nice man—and he is a target. I am going to raise his blind and call many of his raises early in the tournament and try to outplay him. My belief is that he will play predictably. Predictable play is what professionals have for dinner. I want to be a thorn in the side of this player. He is in the two seat and I will typically have position on him, which makes things even better. Before the tournament has started, I've simply glanced at two people and come up with a game plan. By the time I've evaluated all eight of my opponents I have a very clear idea of what I want to do at the table—and the cards are about to go in the air. It's time to Shuffle Up and Deal!

Build Your Stack

Early on, tournament poker is very similar to ring-game poker. There is no concern about eliminating players, or folding to reach the money. The money is days away. Right now, the only concern is increasing your chip count.

Most WPT events start their players with 10,000 in chips and blinds of just 25 and 50. This means you'll see very few preflop all-ins, and a lot of pots won with bets and raises after the flop—postflop fireworks, as I like to say. I tend to play a lot of pots in the first round. This is contrary to some theorists who contend there is no reason to get involved early on. Playing after the flop is the most skillful part of this game. I love this aspect of No Limit Hold 'Em, and I can use my postflop skill far more effectively in the first round than at any other time.

I often raise to just double the blind to 100. I might make it 150 or, in very rare cases, 200. *The point is, I keep my preflop raises small.* This allows me to take control of the pots and learn how my opponents play without committing too many chips in the process. I am more inclined to make a minimum raise from early position than late position. That's because I usually have a pretty good hand when I enter the pot under the gun, and I don't mind a little action. It's really fine with me if I get called. I am confident in my post-flop ability, so it's OK if my small preflop raises encourage callers—especially if those callers are weak players. I am constantly making bets to win pots with or without hands and daring people to call or raise me. This makes me a feared player at the table. Everybody knows I have come to play. With this style I am unpredictable and I give myself a chance to accumulate chips. My opponents get frustrated, and that sometimes causes them to bluff in the wrong spot. And that's how I can finally win a big pot after picking up so many small ones. A good thing about playing a lot of pots is that I will be ready to play when I pick up a big hand. I will probably get action, and I will be armed with a lot of information about my opponents, because I've played so many hands with them already. Overly tight players wait for a big hand, then they pick up two jacks and wonder what to do when an ace flops. They might be beat, they might not, but they'll be afraid to fold because they've waited so long for the big pair that they feel married to it. I will have put myself in marginal situations all day so I'm much prepared for tough decisions. Often the player who rarely plays is as much of a target as the one who always does for exactly the reason I've described. So you might as well play pots and get some chips.

What Hands to Play Early in the Tournament

This brings us to the question of what specific hands you should be playing. I want to play pots, but I don't want to be playing every pot. No one is good enough to pull that off (well, except maybe Phil Ivey). As I said earlier, I am less inclined to enter the pot in early position than late position. I am, however, more inclined to play from early position than a tight player is. When a tight player raises from early position, we can pretty much assume he has a big pair or A-K. Knowing this, I might call him in position with suited connectors, small pairs, or other speculative hands if we both have a lot of chips. This is because if the flop comes with connecting cards, like 7-8-9, I can be sure my opponent doesn't like this flop. There is no hand he would've played from early position so that he likes this flop. I can therefore be aggressive no matter what I have. If my opponent bets and I raise, he may well throw away two aces. And if he doesn't throw them away on the flop, he will probably throw them away on the turn. This is why I play a few more hands from early position. When the flop comes 7-8-9, I want my opponents to think I could have J-10s, or at least a set. This makes it much tougher for them to try to take the pot away from me.

From early position, I'm likely to open-raise with any pair, A-K, or A-Q, and some suited connectors. This way, no matter what flops I'm capable of holding a big hand, but I'm also not getting out of line. I'm still folding the vast majority of my hands under the gun, and when I open, I'm usually opening for a minimum raise. Again, this style makes me dangerous and unpredictable. I'm as likely to have aces as 7-6 suited, and it's up to my opponents to figure out which one I have at any given time.

Let's say I do have the 7-6 suited and I open-raise from early position and get called. If the flop comes with an ace, I'll be able to represent a big ace and will probably force a medium pocket pair to lay down his hand. But if the flop actually hits my hand, with two pair, or trips, or maybe a straight flush draw, I'm going to get real aggressive. I might have a huge hand, or I might have a huge draw, but either way my opponent is in trouble—and he'll have a real hard time putting me on the hand I have.

From middle position, I'll open up my game a little more. I'll throw in hands like A-J and A-10, and probably suited one- and two-gappers like J-9s, or K-10s. Basically, I'll open with any hand that has potential to flop big. I'll be more inclined to open on a weak player's big blind than on a pro's big blind. I'll also open for a slightly larger raise in middle position—probably two-and-a-half to three times the big blind. Since I have a few more weak hands in my range, I'm not quite as eager to get action (although I still don't mind it).

In middle position, I have fewer players to get through, so I don't have to worry quite as much about running into a reraise. Also, if I do get reraised, it's more likely to be a resteal than if I get reraised after raising under the gun. This gives me a few more options on how to play the hand. I'm more inclined to put in the third raise after opening in middle position than I am to do it under the gun. A lot of times that wins me the pot right there. I'm also more comfortable calling a reraise and taking a look at a flop from middle position—especially if the reraise comes from one of the blinds, a player I was probably going after, and looking to get involved with, in the first place. I'll talk more about defending my raises in a few paragraphs.

In late position, I might open with anything. If everyone folds to me on the button, for example, I'll raise a weak player's big blind with almost any two cards. Again, I'm daring him to play a pot with me out of position. Most of the time, he won't want to. When he does, that's OK, too. I'm *looking* for him to take a shot at me, because eventually he's going to take a shot at the wrong time. Whether I choose to open-raise in late position depends less on my cards than on who has the blinds, what my image is at that particular moment, and what the respective stack sizes are. I love to play pots in position, and I'm trying to find reasons to do it with a lot of different hands. Once more, this is in contrast to many players who look for reasons not to get involved. *I look for reasons to get involved.*

When You Get Reraised

Usually when I'm playing my game, I have my opponents doubting the correct course of action and they often end up just calling me almost as a reflex. Sometimes, however, even I get reraised. When this happens, it's time to reassess the situation. Obviously, I'll be inclined to put in the next raise with pocket aces and pocket kings. But I don't want those to be the only hands with which I put in the third raise, or I risk becoming predictable myself (and we never want that). So I'll usually put in the third raise with A-K. A-K is a powerful hand in No Limit Hold 'Em, and one of its best features is that, when you hold it, it's much less likely that your opponent has pocket kings or pocket aces. This puts him in a tough spot when you put in the third raise, even if he has a hand as strong as pocket queens. He may very well fold, there is a chance he'll call, but he almost certainly won't put in the fourth raise unless he has one of the very big pairs. By putting in the third raise with A-K, I stand a good chance of picking up the pot right there, I stand very little chance of facing a tough decision if my opponent raises again, and I avoid being too predictable by only making the third raise with a big pair.

Now, I won't put in the third raise with A-K every time. Especially if I have position and the chips are deep, I may choose to take a flop and just call my opponent's reraise. This also makes it hard for my opponent to put me on A-K when I hit my flop. Sometimes I'll put in the third raise with a speculative hand like J-10 suited. By doing this, I accomplish two things. First, I let my opponent know that I'm not just going to roll over if he decides to raise me. Everyone at the table must know that if they tangle with me, they have to be ready to play for all their chips. Second, it adds a lot of deception if my opponent decides to call my raise and look at a flop. He won't be able to narrow my hands to aces, kings, and A-K, because I'm always capable of making a play with some other holding.

Although I am capable of making that third raise preflop with different hands, very often I like to call raises and reraises before the flop. And as I've said over and over, I much prefer to do this when I have position on my opponents. The reason I like to call a lot, rather than reraise myself, is simple. If my opponent raises, he can always have aces. And if my opponent has aces, I want a chance to outflop him and get all of his chips. If I reraise preflop into my opponent's aces, I'll almost certainly get shut out before we ever see a flop. But if I call preflop, I'll have a chance to use my postflop playing ability. Even if my opponent doesn't have aces, I like to take flops. That's my style for the early rounds, and I've had a lot of success with it. If a tight player raises in middle position, I'm inclined to call on the button with 6-5s. If I raise in early position and a bad player makes a small reraise, I'm inclined to call with whatever opening hand I have. And if I raise on the button and get reraised by the small blind, I'll probably call with suited or connecting cards. I'm looking to play pots, assuming, of course, we all have a lot of chips relative to the blinds (say 100 big blinds or more in each of our stacks). This is how I get chips. This is how I win tournaments.

Be Prepared for Fluctuations

When you play an aggressive style your chip position rarely stays close to the initial stack size. Be prepared for fluctuations. Be ready to see your mountain of chips disappear in one hand. And be ready to see your short stack grow to a tower in a matter of minutes.

When I'm playing a tournament, I try to stay in the moment. This way, I can play when I suddenly find myself shortstacked, even if I've spent the last few hours as a big stack. Similarly, I can go to work as a big stack immediately, even if I've been in short-stack mode for a long time. Let me give you some examples.

Say I have gotten unlucky during the first level and I am now down to $5,000. The blinds are going up to $50–$100, which means there is less room for postflop play. In poker you must adapt to both the players around you and your chip stack. Since I have lost half my starting stack, it's time to shift gears a bit. I am still looking to pick on the weak spots, but my starting hand requirements have tightened. Now I may throw away the 8-7s in early position and lean more towards the big cards all players are familiar with playing. I just don't have enough chips to justify playing speculative hands. I mean, the most I can possibly win from one opponent is 50 big blinds. I'm not going to do that often enough to make the suited connectors playable out of position.

Fast forward another hour. For some inexplicable reason, my stack has dwindled further. Don't these people know who I am! Now the blinds have gone up to $100–$200. There is still no ante, but I've only got $2,000 in my stack. This is, in my opinion, the most awkward stack size to play in all of No Limit Hold 'Em—but it's a stack size most players find themselves holding at least once per tournament. I need to double up, but how do I accomplish this? For example, I pick up A-10 under the gun. With a bigger stack size I might double the blind and hope to use my postflop play. But with only ten blinds in my stack, my options are less clear. I see many players move all-in here. They figure that a standard raise would pot-commit them and they won't fold to a reraise, so why not just move all-in and let whatever happens happen? To me, this is equivalent to giving up. You will get called only by better hands, including bigger aces, making you a big dog, and nearly all pocket pairs. In your best case, you pick up the blinds uncontested, and even if that happens you only pick up 300 chips. I prefer calling, raising to 400 or 500, or even folding the hand to moving all-in. By playing the hand slower, I can disguise my hand and make it look stronger than it is. It also enables me to fold if there is significant action behind me and I am certain I am dominated. The point is to not give up. We are trying to eliminate some of the luck from a game of chance and skill. If you consistently make moves just hoping your opponent has nothing, without leaving yourself an escape route if you're wrong, you will often find yourself out early instead of having a chance to get lucky later. You never know when you are going to get hot, but it does you little good if you're not still in the tournament. There are certainly times when you have no choice but to fold or move in, but many players switch to this "move or muck" mode far too early. When you've got 10 big blinds under the gun, you still have options. You're not dead yet.

Reading Tells

OK, let's back up. This time, instead of losing my chips in the first hour, I have increased my stack to 15,000. I am feeling great and have likely brought my A-game to the table. I probably have a larger stack than any of my opponents, and I control the table. Now is not the time to be content. It is time to stay in the action and try to run my chips up further. Stay focused. If I lose a few pots and people think I'm on tilt, I might slow down a bit. Though I always advocate aggression, it is important to be selective about it. Only the best players in the world can raise every pot and get away with it (and even they don't always get away with it). Try to get in your opponents' heads. What do they think you are up to with your aggressive style? Always reassess your opponents' goals. Are they happy with their chip positions? Are they getting impatient? Which players think you are getting out of line? Constantly evaluate everything at the poker table. If my neighbor is listening to an iPod, I even like to lean over and see what he's listening to. It never hurts to pay attention. I am looking for anything and everything.

Of course, I am looking even more closely at what my opponents do when they're actually playing a hand. Do they gently place their chips in the pot, or do they slam them emphatically? Do they quietly say raise, or are they more boisterous? How do they cut their stacks, and what are their facial expressions when their opponents are contemplating a reraise?

All of these actions are *tells,* physical actions a player takes, consciously or unconsciously, that give away the strength of his hand. It might seem difficult, at first, to interpret any tic or speech or stare you notice at the table. Don't worry, there's actually a science to it.

The pioneer in the field of poker tells was America's self-proclaimed "Mad Genius of Poker"—Mike Caro. Mike was featured on the *World Poker Tour*'s "Poker by the Book" episode and held his own against the likes of tournament professionals Phil Hellmuth, Doyle Brunson, and T. J. Cloutier. *Caro's Book of Poker Tells* introduced the world to the science of tells. I'll explain here what I learned from Mr. Caro.

First of all, don't believe anything anyone says or does at a poker table. Your opponents are almost always putting on an act of some kind, trying to deceive you about the strength of their hands. Caro's central concept is that when analyzing an opponent's action, *strong means weak and weak means strong*. I've definitely noticed this in the cash games and tournaments I play, even World Poker Tour events.

A lot of "weak" actions are, in reality, serious cause for concern at the table. A quiet raise or a sad speech followed by a bet is usually made by somebody holding the nuts. The best is when a player shakes his head in disgust when the flush card comes in, and then proceeds to raise when the action gets to him. Who does he think he's fooling? Any time a player appears to be working at nonchalance, he likely has a monster. If he shrugs his shoulders, or makes a big production out of scratching his head, or suddenly becomes very talkative after he's been quiet all night, he has woken up with a hand, and he just can't help himself from trying to sell it in whatever way he can.

At the same time, almost all of the bravado you see at the poker table is false bravado. All that macho posturing you see—the slamming of chips, the bold, aggressive staredown, the guy who says out loud, "You want to go all-in on this hand!"—is almost always done by a player who is bluffing. If you've watched any of my World Poker Tour final table appearances, you'll see that I don't do these things. I try to stay calm and collected at the table. I've been told I make my bets coolly and with the same Erick Lindgren smile whether I've got deuce-four or pocket aces. I'm not interested in trying to appear macho when I play poker. I'm interested in winning money.

Another trick I learned from Caro is to watch the players, or at least one player, as the flop comes out. You can't fake your first reaction to the flop, and if I can pick up on that first reaction from my opponent, I've got him. One of the most reliable tells I've noticed is the quick glance at chips as the flop comes down. A player who does this *loves* the flop, and just can't wait to stick his chips in the pot. The opposite of this tell is the one where your opponent stares at the flop for several seconds after it's been revealed. This guy has nothing, but he is trying desperately to find something by looking at the flop for as long as he can (either that or he's flopped a royal flush and is double-checking because he just can't believe his luck, but that is a pretty rare occurrence). These are *reaction tells,* and when you spot one, it's as good as gold. You can thank Mike Caro for being the first to figure this out.

Here's one last thing Mike taught me about spotting a bluff. Bluffing makes people uncomfortable, nervous. When people bluff, they are afraid they're going to get called. So the more relaxed a person seems, the better his hand usually is. A bluffer might hold his breath, without realizing he's doing it, because it's a natural instinct to hold your breath when things get uncomfortable. If you get a bluffer to talk, he might blabber on in a mostly incomprehensible way. He's too nervous to put an actual sentence together. On the other hand, a guy who's chatting or breathing, or even singing after he makes a bet, is usually comfortable with his situation in the poker universe. That guy has a hand. A player who *stops* talking, or breathing, or humming, however, is a player you might want to call down. These are *comfort tells.* They're harder to spot, but pretty damn useful in their own right.

I pick up more tells on inexperienced players than I do on professionals, but occasionally even good players will have tells. The trick is, you usually have to prod them a little. If you get them off their game, even the best players will start giving away information at the table. I'll give you two examples of where I used a tell, one against a weak player, and one against a pro.

Getting Information

This first hand happened at a Bellagio tournament in 2004. I drew a very good first table and recognized only two faces. They were solid pros, but neither was overly aggressive. I knew I could take control of the table and quickly looked around to find the best targets. I noticed an older man in a cowboy hat who had been involved in too many pots, and decided he was my mark. My plan was to bluff him the first chance I got, or to do whatever I could to get under his skin. I wanted him to view me as a young hotshot, hoping he'd eventually try to bully me at the wrong time (for him).

I chopped away at some small pots (a lot of small pots, in fact) and my $20,000 starting stack grew to $43,000 when Cowboy and I finally got to lock horns. I'd been raising a lot of hands, so it was nothing new when I opened for $1,200 with the blinds at $200–$400. I had two jacks in my hand. I got three callers, including Cowboy in the big blind. The flop came 7h-4c-4h and the small blind checked. It was Cowboy's turn, and he pushed all-in. He looked proud, firing his $37,000 into a $5,000 pot.

I was completely befuddled. What was going on? The bet

made no sense any way I looked at it, but that's not enough reason to call. I had to be almost entirely sure I had the best hand if I was going to call an overbet as large as that one. There was a player to act behind me, but he only had $3,000. He wasn't going to matter much in this hand. My best hope in this situation was to get Cowboy to talk. "Why'd you bet so much?" I asked. He told me to call and find out. Bingo. False bravado.

So I knew he was weak, but weak in this situation could still have meant two queens. I made a mental list of his possible hands: A-x hearts for the nut flush draw. Pocket eights, maybe. Maybe a somewhat bigger pair, but almost certainly not aces or kings. Or a random berzerko bet with a pair of sevens. Of all the hands he could have, and there were a lot of hands I thought he could have, only the two queens beat me. After a minute or two of deliberation, I called. He flipped up 10-7 for one pair! He failed to improve, and I suddenly found myself with $80,000 in chips and ready to roll.

On Day Two of that same tournament, I started as the chip leader at my table, with more than double the average stack. But I had a tougher table than I'd had on Day One, with professionals Annie Duke, Bill Gazes, Casey Kastle, and Lee Salem all joining in the party.

An older guy at the table started raising and reraising a lot of pots, and generally played wildly. Like the Cowboy from a day earlier, he was definitely the mark. He got Casey, who was stuck on his right, especially frustrated. The three times Casey brought it in for a raise, the old man reraised and Casey threw his hand away. On this hand, Casey limped in for $1,200. Annie, Lee, and another player all called.

I was pretty sure I had the best hand with my A-10, and I raised it $5,000. I expected to win the pot right there, and I was rather surprised and unhappy when Casey quickly said, "All-in," for a total bet of $25,000. It was folded back to me, and I was faced with a decision for half my chips.

Here, Casey was representing that he limped in with A-A hoping for a raise behind him so he could reraise all-in. This is a typical slow play in No Limit Hold 'Em. But his play here didn't make sense. Wouldn't Casey have been more than happy to raise with his A-A, knowing the older gentleman would reraise him? I looked at Casey hoping to get a read, but he was frozen like a kid playing statue.

I needed more information, so I tried to get Casey to acknowledge that I was still in the hand, or at the very least, that he was still alive. I asked if he limped with aces, but I still got no reaction. I then said, "Can you beat queen-high?" He finally looked up, smirked, and said, "Yeah, I can beat queen-high."

As I said earlier, some people in poker like to lie about their hands. Here, it felt like Casey was happy to be able to tell the truth in response to what was, admittedly, a pretty silly question. After all, if I couldn't beat queen-high, why was I even thinking of calling? But it was the way Casey gave his answer that brought me to my read. It was as though he was relieved I had mentioned queen-high—because he had precisely king-high!

Now I felt certain that Casey held K-T, K-J, or K-Q suited. I had him. "I'm not buying it," I said as I pushed in my chips. "Good call," he said as he turned over K-10 of diamonds. I proudly showed my A-10 and it held up, winning me the $50,000 pot. Sometimes a simple question can return a very profitable answer. Just remember not to fall into the trap of giving away information yourself. You may not want to try to pry information from the pros until you have some experience doing it against the amateurs.

This Is Not Easy Money

If this sounds complicated, it is. Poker at its highest level is very tough and totally exhausting. As hard as you try to stay focused, I promise there will be times you fade out and lose your concentration. Be honest with yourself and try to make fewer moves when you are tired, but do whatever you can to be alert again. Even more important, gauge how your opponents are handling the long and grueling day. Believe it or not, many players just want to double up or go home before Day One comes to an end. These are the people you want to trap. Let them bluff off all their chips to you. Maintain your composure throughout the tournament and you will see people blow up all around you, losing their stacks.

The early stage of the tournament is about a lot of things. It's about gathering information about your opponents. It's about establishing your own image. It's about collecting chips. It's not about avoiding confrontations. If you can get yourself in a favorable position to earn a whole bunch of chips, you should do it, even if it means risking elimination from the event. After a few hours of poker at a World Poker Tour event, you should know how all your opponents play, you should have a well-thought-out game plan, and you will (we hope) have enough chips to be a concern for everyone else at the table.

CHAPTER FOUR

Playing after the Flop

They say the person who invented money was smart, but the person who invented poker chips was a genius. Well, the person who invented poker was smart, but the person who invented the flop deserves a Nobel Prize. The flop is the reason Hold 'Em is so popular. How can anyone resist the flop? You get three cards at once! Any hand can win if you get the next three cards at once! Players calling "to look at a flop" are among the biggest reasons I've been able to make a living at this game. In a lot of ways, the flop is where the poker begins.

Postflop Strategy

In the last chapter, I said over and over again that I like to take flops against weaker opposition. My entire preflop strategy is based on the idea that I can outplay most of my opponents after the flop. Now is the time to show you how I do that.

Postflop play is far more nuanced, situational, and read-dependent than preflop play. Before the flop, you're usually just playing your cards. After the flop, you have a lot more information to work with, and it becomes possible to significantly narrow down your opponent's range of hands. *After the flop, you're playing the player.* This is why the best strategy for beginning players is often to make big raises and reraises before the flop. Most opponents will be afraid to commit against those big raises without big pairs, and if someone does finally take a shot at this beginner, the beginner won't have to worry much about postflop play because a good chunk of the money will have gone in preflop. Experienced players, on the other hand, like to keep the pot small before the flop. As you know by now, I make a lot of small raises preflop, daring my opponents to call me and take a flop with me. And if a new player wants to take a shot at me with a big reraise, I'll eventually either trap him with a big pair, or come over the top of him preflop for all his chips. I would prefer to take flops, but if my opponents aren't letting me, I'm not just going to get run over.

Usually, though, people are reluctant to play back at me preflop, and I end up taking a lot of flops cheaply in the early stages of a tournament. How does this work to my advantage? Well here's another secret—I'm not the greatest postflop player ever, it's just that most of my opponents aren't as good as I am! Yup, just as in virtually every other aspect of poker, you make the most money after the flop not from your own brilliant play, but from your opponents' mistakes.

There are a ton of things inexperienced players do after the flop that will cost themselves chips in the long run. They give off tells, they don't understand the value of their hands, they slowplay when they shouldn't, they let themselves get trapped, they make overly tight folds, they make overly loose calls. You name it, they do it. It takes a lot of time and ability for good players to learn not to make such mistakes. Let me list some of the most common postflop mistakes I see new players make.

1. Overvaluing big pocket pairs, especially AA. If you don't flop a set with your big pair, then you have a very vulnerable hand after the flop. You have only one pair, and you could easily be smashed. It's amazing how many players don't understand this. In one WPT event where we all started with $20,000 in chips, I saw a player put in his entire stack with pocket aces on a board of 6-6-4, when there was only $500 in the pot to start the hand (the pocket aces did not raise before the flop). Of course, the other guy had a six and the aces went broke.

There are some players who will not only call any bet with two aces in their hand, but will raise and reraise with them on any flop. These are usually inexperienced players, the ones who don't always act in turn, or fail to state their intention to raise, or just look nervous. Try to take a flop cheaply against these players, and if you flop a hand that beats aces, be prepared to put in all your chips.

In fact, when the stacks are deep, I usually *want* my opponent to have aces, especially if he's a bad player, but even if he's a good player. The fact of the matter is, it's very difficult for anyone to play unimproved aces after the flop. You can't just check and fold with them every time, or I will rob you to death. At the same time, you're a total sucker if you constantly get all your chips in with them, as I've just described. So it's a very fine line, and even a lot of good players have problems toeing it. Personally, I like to get passive with aces if I'm not sure where I stand. I might check and call with them on both the flop *and* the turn, figuring I'm either way ahead or way behind, so why not let my opponent do the betting in either case? This is difficult strategy to execute, however, and not everyone does it. When an early position player raises, and I call on the button with two sixes, I'm hoping he has aces. I'm praying he has aces. My implied odds when I hit my set are just so much greater when he does. This is another reason I open-raise in early position with many hands other than aces. I don't want my opponents to just assume they can get paid off every time they flop a monster.

A lot of players are hoping their opponent might have 5-5 or ace-deuce when they call a raise in position with two 6s. My question to those players is, how can you get paid against those hands? Always root for your opponents to have aces.

2. Overbetting the pot. Some players will habitually bet way too much money when compared to the size of the pot. They'll bet two or three times what's in the pot in an effort to win it. The problem is, these players are risking far too much to win too little. Their overbets will win the pot most of the time, but the times they fail often mean elimination from the tournament. Overbettors are asking to be trapped. Keep seeing flops cheaply against them, and eventually they will bet off all their money to you.

3. Underbetting the pot. Limit Hold 'Em players who are giving No Limit Hold 'Em a shot for the first time often make Limit Hold 'Em bets. If the blinds are $100 and $200, these players usually bet $200 on the flop, even if the pot has $2,000 or $3,000 in it. There are many ways to take advantage of such a player. First, you can call with just about any speculative hand (gut-shot straight draw, bottom pair, any pocket pair) hoping to make a big hand and earn a lot of money from your opponent on the later streets. Alternatively, you can get aggressive against the mini-bettor by bluff-raising. Usually, a bluff-raise requires you to commit a lot of chips, which is why it's a somewhat rare play. But against the mini-bettor, a bluff-raise costs basically the same amount that a typical bet would. The great thing is, it looks like you have a very strong hand. That's because you're *raising*—you are taking an aggressive action against another player who has shown interest in the pot. This automatically shows greater strength than betting does, even though in this case it doesn't cost very much. The Limit Hold 'Em bettor's small wager allows you a much better chance to take down the pot on the flop, with almost no increased risk.

4. Slow-playing. There is a class of aggressive players who always bet when they have a medium-strength hand or worse, but always check their monsters. I love these people. I can raise their bets liberally, but when they check I can be sure something is up. Whenever these guys bet, I always have the option to raise, because I know they would never bet out with their very strong hands. And when these guys check, I know I always have the opportunity to win a big pot if my opponent manages to check me into the nuts. So many players take this backward approach of checking their good hands and betting their bad ones, and these players are fueling the poker economy. Avoid this mistake yourself by sometimes betting both your monsters and your bluffs, and by sometimes checking your bad hands.

5. Giving up too early. I played in a World Poker Tour event with a guy who would raise with A-K before the flop, and then check the flop every single time he missed. He went so far as to show his A-K and shake his head in resignation as he folded to his opponent's bet. "I never win with that hand," he would say. Well, once I saw this, I started calling his raises a lot, planning to bet the flop anytime he checked to me. This tactic worked great. I love those guys, too, the players who raise a lot preflop and often check-fold later on. I let them build up my pots, and then I take them away with just one bet.

As I said, these are just some of the numerous mistakes inexperienced players make, but they are also some of the most common mistakes and the most profitable (for us). Being aware of these mistakes will immediately make you a stronger No Limit Hold 'Em player. But to be a truly great No Limit Hold 'Em player, you have to know more than what not to do.

Knowing What Hands to Play

For starters, you need to know what a good hand is. I've already said an unimproved A-A is not a good hand on the flop when you have a lot of chips in front of you. It's not a bad hand, but it's also not necessarily a hand you would be looking to get all-in with. A good hand is one that you would happily call your opponent's all-in wager with if you were given the opportunity. So what are good hands on the flop? Well, obviously, top set (three of a kind of the highest card on the board) is a good hand, as is a straight or the nut flush. In fact, most any set is a good hand. If you never folded a set on the flop in No Limit Hold 'Em, you probably wouldn't be making too much of a mistake. In addition, most any flush is a good hand, although a small flush is actually not as good as a small set. If your small flush is behind, you never have any redraws. If a set is losing to a straight or a flush, at least the board can pair and give you a full house. These definitions of "good hands" assume you are in a heads-up pot. To overcall an all-in on the flop in No Limit Hold 'Em, after two players with deep stacks have both committed all their chips, you usually need the nuts (just as you would need A-A to call in that situation pre-flop). Fortunately, most No Limit pots are contested heads-up.

I don't think too many readers will be surprised that sets, straights, and flushes are big hands in No Limit Hold 'Em. But there are some other hands that are also very strong, and they might not be obvious to even experienced players. The hands I'm talking about are straight flush draws, or hands that contain a straight draw and a flush draw. Some examples are Jh-Th on a board of 9h-8h-3c, or As-7s on a board of 9s-8s-6h, or 9d-8d on a board of 5d-7h-Jd. In all of these examples, we have 15 outs (9 cards that complete our flush, and 6 offsuit cards that complete our straight) even if our opponent has a set. The great thing about straight flush draws is that they are *never* that far behind. And that means you should often be willing to raise all-in with these draws. I'll explain why.

If everyone has a lot of chips, the only hand it makes sense to raise all-in with preflop is two aces. This is because with any other hand, you always risk running into aces and finding yourself an enormous underdog. The flip side of that is you yourself would almost never move-in with aces preflop for a big overbet, because no worse hand is supposed to call you. But on the flop, it does make sense to raise all-in with straight flush draws, because you can never get trapped as a big underdog. Even if your opponent has the nuts, you have a reasonable chance (sometimes as high as 42 percent!) to win the hand. And here's the best part. If you play your sets and straight flush draws the same way—very aggressively—your opponent won't know what to do when you move in. Do you have the nuts, or do you have a monster draw? If you have the nuts and get called, fantastic. If you have a monster draw and get called, that's not too big a deal. Not only do you have a ton of outs, but you're much more likely to get action on all of your hands in the future. Are you starting to see why I love postflop play in No Limit Hold 'Em?

The only downside of straight flush draws is that it's not always possible to have them. On a rainbow board of K-7-2, if you move-in with your set of kings, it's going to be hard for your opponent to think, "Hmm, he might have a straight flush draw," and call you. He won't think this because there are no straight or flush draws on that flop! This leads to my next point: the more possible draws on the board, the bigger your bets should be. There are several reasons for this. First, if you bet too small on a board with a lot of draws, it will be very correct for your opponent with a draw to call you. Second, on a ragged, rainbow board, you are going to be either way ahead or way behind when you bet. There is no draw you might be up against where you're only slightly ahead. Either you have very few outs, or your opponent does. If you're way ahead, you want to keep your opponent around, so you should bet small. If you're way behind, you want to find out as cheaply as possible, so you should bet small. Hey, a small bet makes sense either way! Finally, as I illustrated earlier, there are many hands you could have on a draw-heavy board where you'd be inclined to go all-in, so you're OK making big bets on the way there. On a ragged, rainbow board, you pretty much need a set to raise all-in, and it's not too likely you'll have one. You should make small bets on rainbow boards to protect yourself all those times when you *don't* have a set.

Difference Between Small and Big Bets

I guess I should tell you what I mean by small bets and large bets. After the flop, bet sizes are measured in relation to the pot. A small bet is half the pot or less. A large bet would be about the size of the pot. I almost never overbet the pot, unless a standard bet would commit me to the pot, in which case I would just move all-in instead. This way I never get too trapped if I'm bluffing, and I also give my opponent the chance to call those times when I want him or her to call. When I want to bet, I bet about half the pot on ragged boards, and about the size of the pot on boards with a bunch of draws. By playing this way, I constantly keep my opponents guessing, and that's exactly what I want them to do. I don't ever want my playing style to give away my hand.

Playing Your Position

There is an important aspect to postflop play that I haven't yet touched on in this chapter, but that I certainly mentioned many times earlier in the book, and that is *position*. I have so many more options when I have position. If my opponent checks, I can take a free card, or I can try to win the pot with a bet. If my opponent bets, I can fold and get out cheaply, I can raise and try to scoop a big pot, or I can just call and see what happens on the turn. If I'm first to act, I'm in a much tougher spot. I can never be sure I'm getting a free card, I have little-to-no information about my opponent's hand when I'm deciding to bet, and if I choose to check-call, I have to act first *again* on the next betting round. Clearly, there are many advantages to playing pots in position, which is why I'm much more inclined to call raises preflop from the button or cutoff than from anywhere else. When I'm out of position, I'm more likely to play "reraise or fold" preflop. This gives me more information on how to go about playing the rest of the hand, and reduces my opponent's positional advantage by getting more money into the pot before the flop.

Sometimes, however, even I end up taking flops when I am out of position. Playing out of position is one of the hardest things to do in No Limit Hold 'Em, but it can be done. The key is to find a way to take control of the hand. Sometimes you do this by betting, sometimes by inducing your opponent to bet. Either way, if you have a clear idea about what your goal is for the hand, you will be able to show a profit playing pots when acting first.

Here's one example of how I take control of a hand when first to act. Say I've called a raise from the big blind with 8-6s and I flop a flush draw. I have a hand I'd like to play, but if I check, my opponent is likely to make a decent-sized bet that I won't want to call. My only options will be to check-raise or fold. I might sometimes check-raise, but then I would be committing a lot of chips to a semi-bluff without knowing much about my opponent's hand. Not only that, I'll only win a big pot if my opponent calls my bet *and* I hit my flush. If he reraises, I probably have to fold, and if he folds, that's fine, but I might have missed an opportunity to win a bigger pot by hitting a flush on him. Because of this, I've come up with an alternative play to check-raising the flush draw, and that play is betting out for a small amount. This bet often stuns my opponents into calling (or even folding) in spots where they would've almost definitely bet if I had checked. Now I actually have a chance to draw at my flush for a small price, when my opponent flat-calls my bet. If my opponent decides to raise, I've only lost the small bet I made, and I can still reraise if I really want to. I love the small lead-out bet with a draw. It's a great way to control the pot out of position, and when you do hit your hand on the turn it's usually well disguised. And, of course, I'll also make the small lead-out with the nuts, so my opponent can never be sure what my bets mean.

I'll give you another example. Say I'm in the big blind and I've called a late position raise with K-J. The flop comes king-high with no likely draws. What do I do? If my opponent has A-K or K-Q I'm toast, but if my opponent has A-Q, A-J, Q-Q, J-J, 10-10, or 9-9, he's in a lot of trouble. There are a lot of hands he could have that I beat, but if I bet out he's very likely to fold them. If I check instead, he's probably going to bet 90 percent of the time or more. So if I bet, I get called or raised when I'm behind, and when I'm ahead my opponent almost always folds.

That sounds like a good reason to check! And that's what I usually do. I let my opponent bluff. Then a lot of time I'll call and let
him bluff again on the turn. If he checks behind on the turn, he
might look me up with a middle pair when I make a small bet on
the river. Sometimes I'll check-raise the flop, but not usually. It's
another one of the situations where I'm either way ahead or way
behind. It's OK, and often preferable, to play passively in that scenario. It might not look like I'm controlling the hand by check-
calling, but I am. A lot of times I know what my opponent is
going to do before he does. I'm inducing him to bluff, and I have
a hand to snap him off with. Yes, I'll lose money to A-K by playing this way. But I'm going to lose money to A-K on this flop no
matter what. By playing the way I do, I might lose slightly more
to A-K than an aggressive approach would, but I make a lot more
money against all of the hands I have beaten.

One argument I sometimes hear against checking in this situation is that checking doesn't give you any information. I dis-
agree. If you bet out and get raised, you have some information
but not much. A lot of players read the lead-out bet as sign of
weakness and raise it liberally. In fact, I myself made a mistake of
leading out into an aggressive player at a WPT final (which I'll
get into in detail in chapter 7). But if you check and call and then
check the turn, especially if you're normally aggressive, your opponent's next action will tell you *a lot* about the strength of his
hand. Think about it. What looks scarier—a good player who
calls a raise preflop and then leads out at a ragged flop, or a good
player who calls a raise preflop and then check-calls the flop? To
put it another way, which of these actions is more consistent with
a big hand? In my opinion, checking the flop is a better way to
get information than leading the flop. And it's cheaper, too.

Inducing bluffs is one of the most underrated ways of making
money in No Limit Hold 'Em. Watch Andy Bloch at either of

the two World Poker Tour final tables he's made. He checks and calls against his opponents until they've bluffed off all their money to him. You can't have any fear in this game. People usually interpret that to mean you have to stay aggressive. It is important to play aggressive, but you also can't be afraid to call, if that's your best play. Matt and I have made a lot of money by getting our opponents to bet our hands for us.

Playing the River

I've given you detailed guidelines on how to construct a successful strategy that will work for you on the flop and the turn early in World Poker Tour events. But there is one betting round I haven't touched on yet that deserves some more attention—and that round is the river.

The river is a different animal. There are no more draws, no more bets to make draws pay, and no more semi-bluffs. At the river, you either have the best hand or you don't. There is no question of how far behind or ahead you are. It's all or nothing. Because of this, many players go into a shell and check the river with all but their monsters and their complete busts. Don't be one of those players. There are many other ways to make money by betting the river. Let's look at them.

In general, there are two major reasons to bet the river—to get a worse hand to call (a value bet) or to get a better hand to fold (a bluff). As you can probably guess, I recommend making the same size bet with your value bets as you do with your bluffs, so you don't give your opponents any information. If you like to make large-sized bluffs, then make large-sized bets with your big hands too. And if you like to try to milk your big hands with smallish bets, then bluff occasionally with small bets as well. A lot of players are afraid to value bet hands like two pair or even small sets on the river. They check behind, fearing they are getting trapped by the nuts. I sometimes value-bet one pair on the river, when I just know in my heart that my opponent is going to pay me off with a worse pair. That's what happens when you're an aggressive player—you start finding more and more ways to make money. Anytime you enter the river thinking you had the best hand, and your opponent checks to you, you should consider betting for value. This game is tough enough as it is, and you don't want to leave money on the table by missing bets. I love having people pay me off. I make a lot of money value-betting.

Of course, I bluff, too. If I sense weakness and I think a bluff will work a decent percentage of the time, I try a bluff. It actually doesn't have to work all that often for the bluff to make sense. Say my opponent checks, and I bet half the pot as a bluff. If this play works more than one time in three, I show a profit. That's because every time it works, I win twice as much as I lose when it fails. I often make bets of about half the size of the pot on the river. Sometimes, though, I make much bigger bets. For example, if the board is A-A-A-K-J, and I've decided to bet, I probably have quad aces, or absolutely nothing. Either way, I want to bet big. I want to try to make a huge pot with my quads, or I want to give aces full (or kings full, or jacks full) every reason to fold. In both cases, it makes sense for me to make a large bet, probably around the size of the pot.

Just as most players don't value-bet often enough on the river, most players don't bluff often enough on the river either. Whenever you're against a player who likes to call all the way with draws, you should consider betting the river if your hand can't beat a busted draw. Whenever you have any doubt about whether your opponent truly likes his hand, you should fire out a bet of about half the pot. As I explained, it only has to work one time in three to be successful.

There is one other bet on the river that I don't see very often but is very powerful, and that's the small lead-out with a marginal hand. This bet is not a value bet, because it won't usually get called by a worse hand, and it's not a bluff because it will almost never get a better hand to fold, but it still makes sense. The idea is that you take the bluff away from your opponent. Most players are much more inclined to bluff than to bluff-raise. By betting small with a mediocre made hand like one small pair, you often prevent your opponent from bluffing you out of the pot. And if you do get raised, you can now be much more confident that your hand is no good and usually fold with no regrets. So two good things can happen with your small bet—you can avoid getting bluffed out, or you can avoid paying off a big hand with a big bet. It's true that sometimes you want to induce a big-bet bluff with a marginal hand by checking it, and if you're confident in your read of the opponent you should do just that. But if your read is a little less clear, try a weak lead. It's worked very well for me. Of course, you should sometimes make this small lead-out with the nuts as well. This will prevent the top players from figuring out what you're doing, and taking away your play with a bluff-raise.

Putting It All Together

Here are some examples of postflop plays I made in a recent WPT event that illustrate these ideas.

In level one, with the blinds at $50 and $100, and with most players still at their 20,000-chip starting stack, I made it 300 with king-jack offsuit in middle position. I got called by one of the many longtime professional poker players making the jump into No Limit Hold 'Em tournaments. He was sitting a few seats to my left. The flop came 10-5-6 with two spades and I bet out 600.

My opponent called. The turn brought the jack of spades, and I decided to check. My opponent bet $1,300 and I called. I didn't have a spade. This is a perfect example of a situation where if I chose to bet, my opponent would probably fold all worse hands and call or raise with all better ones. That's a great time to induce a bluff, and so I did—thinking I would call him down all the way. The river brought a king of spades, making me two pair, but putting four dangerous spades on board. I checked, and my opponent fired $1,800 into the pot. After some deliberation I folded and he showed me A-5, no spade. This was a situation where a weak lead on the river would've given me an excellent chance to win the pot. But I knew this player wanted to bluff against me, and so I induced him to continue bluffing. For some reason I got discouraged at the river card and didn't go with my read. That's not the way to play poker, but even those of us who play poker for a living make mistakes. I had a plan, I was perfectly willing to execute that plan, and then I just didn't. It takes more than a good plan to get the money in this game—you've got to be able to pull the trigger as well. A hand like this one, early in the tournament, fought over a relatively small pot, is the kind of hand you don't see on television. But hands like this one are what poker is all about.

Soon afterward, the following hand came up. We were missing a few players from our 10-handed table, as some people were late to the tournament. Absent players have to post blinds just as if they were at the table (although obviously the dealer or another player does the physical posting for them). These absent-player blinds often get attacked by aggressive players because of the built-in overlay. I had such an aggressive player on my right—Minneapolis Jim Meehan. Jim was two off the button and raised the $100 blind to $450. It was a big raise, and naturally I was looking for an excuse to play. I looked down at the 10-4 of hearts and decided to go ahead and make a loose call. I wanted to see if I could win the pot by flopping a hand, or stealing without one. The flop came 7-6-4 rainbow and Jim somewhat surprisingly checked. I bet $700 and he called me quickly. The turn was a jack and Jim checked again. I decided to check as well. I felt Jim had something like A-8 in his hand, giving him two overcards and a gutshot on the flop, but I wasn't sure. There was still a chance I was being trapped. Again, checking kept the pot small, allowed me to take a free card to improve my lackluster hand, and also gave a signal for Jim to bluff on the end.

The river came a three, putting four-to-a-straight on the board. This was not a good turn of events, but I still expected Jim to check. Instead he bet $1,800 at the $2,450 pot. My first instinct was to fold, but I took my time and considered all the information before I acted. Would Jim really have checked a hand with a five in it on the flop? He was an aggressive player, and check-calling with an open-end straight draw didn't fit his mold. The most likely hand he would check and call with was something like A-8, which I could beat. It was also hard to put Jim on two pair. He would've had to raise preflop with a very strange hand, and then check-call the flop with a pair and a straight draw. It wasn't likely. Finally, I couldn't imagine Jim would bet a jack for value in this situation. What worse hand would he expect to call his bet? I decided to call and Jim showed Q-8. I took down the nice pot, and I got the added value of having Jim and everyone else at the table know that I came to play that day.

Here's a hand I played later in the tournament against America's Mad Genius of Poker, Mike Caro. We were at level three, with blinds of $100–$200 and a $25 ante, and we were playing 10-handed. Having 10 players at the table means you can wait longer to pick up a good hand. It also means the likelihood of a player holding a big hand behind you is better than it would be with fewer players. That being said, I hadn't played a hand in some time so I "nuisance-raised" (my term for a minimum raise—it's a nuisance for my opponents, and that's why I like it) to $400 with the queen-deuce of diamonds. I was happy when the easy-to-read small blind called. The big blind called as well, and his name was Mike "the Mad Genius" Caro. This was my first battle against Mike in my career. As the reader knows by now, Mike has done a lot of work to educate poker players, myself included, and I was excited to play a hand with him. Poker is, after all, supposed to be fun.

The flop came J-10-7, with two of my diamonds. Both players checked, and neither looked that interested in playing the hand. Typically, I would bet 75 percent of the pot or so and hope to take it right there. But poker is a game of shifting gears, and I decided to check the flop. If I hit the diamond, both opponents would probably think I had nothing. And I could always try to steal the pot later if I wanted to. The turn brought an offsuit queen, giving me top pair along with my flush draw. Again both players checked. This time I bet $1,100. The small blind folded and Mike made it $5,100. I only had $11,100 left.

His check-raise was strange, to say the least, especially considering I had read him as weak on the flop. One of the hands most players would raise with preflop, and then check on a J-10-7 flop, is exactly A-K. I realized this was an opportunity to represent A-K, which happened to be the nuts on this board, by moving all-in. This would give Mike an opportunity to fold a hand better than mine. It would even be hard for Mike to call with a lower straight, as calling a $6,000 raise would've left him very short. So I pushed all-in.

He thought for a bit, and then folded. I showed him the deuce of diamonds. Showing a card like that after a huge bet is a lot of fun, as it leaves your opponent and the rest of the table speculating out loud about your other card. And if your opponent happened to fold a winner, there is a chance he won't recover for the rest of the tournament (although I wouldn't expect such a fate to befall a great poker authority like Mike Caro).

You now have all the tools at your disposal to build a stack in the early stages of the tournament. After reading this chapter, you might find yourself entering Day Two of a World Poker Tour event as one of the chip leaders! Congratulations if that happens to you. You're about halfway home.

It is vital, however, to understand how to carry your stack through the middle stages of the tournament, when the blinds are much bigger relative to the stacks, and most of the postflop play has been eliminated. The next chapter will show you how that's done.

Chapter Five

Middle Stages of the Tournament

I get a good night's sleep after Day One of a World Poker Tour event. It's easy. I've expended so much energy evaluating and reevaluating my opponents all day in the course of building up my stack that I'm dog tired when I'm done. It's a good thing I'm tired too, since the second day will often sort out the title contenders from the people who are just happy to be there. Day Two is an opportunity to put yourself in fantastic position—a position so strong you'll be a virtual lock to make money in the tournament, and you'll have an excellent chance to win the whole thing. Remember, winning is our goal. Even if you're en-

Erick with PPT commentators Mark Seif and Matt Corboy

tering Day Two short-stacked, don't despair. Don't ever despair. As long as you have chips in front of you, you have a chance to win. Of course this does *not* mean you should play conservatively when you have very few chips. Reread chapter 2 if you need further reinforcement of that idea.

Finishing with a Workable Chip Stack

It's always good to have goals, and to have a plan for how to reach those goals. Your goal on Day Two is to finish with an above-average stack relative to the remaining players. To meet that goal, you'll need to pick up far more than your fair share of pots. A lot of people are going to bust on Day Two, which means the players who don't bust will have a lot more chips than they started with. You'll have to decide which players are tightening up too much, and go after their blinds. You'll have to figure out which players are raising too much, and come over the top of them every once in a while. And if you're lucky enough to get dealt a premium hand, you'll have to find a way to get paid off. Day Two is when the adrenaline rush really kicks in, and if you can negotiate your way through it, you'll be in position to become the WPT's next millionaire. Has a nice ring to it, doesn't it!

If you're interested in becoming an above-average stack, you should first figure out what the average stack size actually is. You don't have to be a math genius to do it. First, calculate the total chips in play by multiplying the starting stack by the number of entrants. Then divide that amount by the number of players remaining, and voilà! You have the average stack size. You can do this for any number of players remaining, so you can figure the average stack size for the final table, the final three tables, whatever you want. What I recommend is that at the start of Day Two, guess how many players will be remaining at day's end (if it's a fixed number, great), and use that number to figure what the average stack size will be going into Day Three. Knowing this information will give you a better idea about when you need to start making moves, and when you should start expecting your shortstacked opponents to make their moves.

Chip Positions

OK, so on Day Two you arrive at the table with a clear idea of what your chip stack should look like by the end of play that night. The next thing you do is look around and memorize the approximate chip positions (short stack, medium stack, or big stack) of all the players at your table. This will be vital in helping determine who will be pot-committed when you raise his blind, and who won't be. It also might affect the way your opponents play. Some players get superaggressive with a big stack, and some players get too conservative with a short stack. Some players are exactly the opposite. Incidentally, your own stack size shouldn't be that important. For any play, you should be making it because you believe that in the long run you'll make more money playing that way than you would any other way. Having a big stack doesn't give you license to make plays that will cost you money, and having a small stack doesn't mean you should pass up opportunities to make money. Your opponents, however, often misuse their stacks. So if you find yourself a big stack and the small stacks keep folding, by all means raise the small stacks every hand. You don't do this because your stack justifies it, you do it because the small stacks are playing badly.

Once the cards are in the air, the first thing you'll notice is that the blinds are substantial. Let's say they are $500-$1,000, and I've got $25,000 in my stack. To give further detail to this hypothetical table, let's say the three players to my right have about the same chips as I do, but the two players to my left are short, each with less than $10,000. The player three to my left has a large stack of $50,000. There will be a big difference in how I will play against a raise from the short stacks, the middle stack, and the big stack.

If one of the short stacks raises to $3,000, I have to assume he'll put in the rest of his chips if I reraise. He's committed to his hand, because he's putting in a third of his chips. It's a rare player who will put in that much of his stack, and then fold to a preflop reraise. If I reraise the short stack, I have to count on getting called. For that reason, I'll occasionally just call a short stack's raise, hoping he'll completely miss the flop and not feel quite so committed to his hand at that point.

If a medium stack raises to $3,000, now *I'm* in an awkward spot. If I choose to reraise, I'll be the one who's pot-committed, since I have to put in $9,000 or so to make a reraise my opponent will respect, but that will leave me with only about $16,000 behind. So a reraise costs more than a third of my stack, and it will be very hard for me to get away (if I want to) when my opponent sets me all-in. So if I choose to reraise a middle stack, I might just move all-in myself and be done with it. Or I might just call the middle stack's raise instead. I don't like to move all my chips in preflop except as a last resort. When I have to, I have to, but if I don't have to commit myself with a reraise, I don't mind just calling and taking a look at a flop.

If I only have $25,000 when a large stack raises, I pretty much have the same problems I have when a medium stack raises. But let's say I've doubled up to $50,000 and now I'm a large stack as well. In this case, when another large stack opens for $3,000, I have a lot of good options available. I can reraise to $9,000 without being pot-committed, I can call and look at a flop, or I can fold and move on. The large stacks are the only opponents against whom I have enough chips to play some postflop poker, which you know by now I love to do. So if I choose to reraise a large stack, it's because I respect that particular opponent's postflop play, or it's because I want to make sure the pot is played heads-up, or it's because I have a monster and I'm trying to represent a steal-raise.

Stealing vs. Defending

Now that I've outlined the stack size considerations that go into every decision I make at the table, let's look at some of those decisions and see how they would play out. At this stage, most of your decisions fall into one of two categories: should I steal, or should I defend? If you have a big hand, you know you're going to raise and/or reraise as the situation warrants. The difficulty comes from knowing how to play medium-strength hands. Stealing the blinds and antes at this stage of the tournament is crucial—much more so than early in the tournament when the

antes didn't even exist. Let's say, for example, that you have
$20,000 and the blinds are $500 and $1,000 with a $100 ante. At
a nine-handed table, stealing the blinds and antes increases your
stack size by 12 percent. Compare that to the beginning of the
tournament when stealing the blinds doesn't even increase your
stack size by 1 percent. Stealing pots is important; the difficulty is
in knowing how to do it.

Here are some of the factors, in order, that you should take
into account when deciding whether to go after someone's
blind.

1. Your position. If you have to get through the entire
table to steal the blinds, you have to play tighter than you
would on the button. There's no way around this. You can
still occasionally raise from UTG with a mediocre hand, but
you can't do it nearly as often as you can from other positions. Remember, against nine opponents, there's about a
25 percent chance that someone else has been dealt queens,
kings, aces, or A-K. You can be the best steal-raiser in the
world, and you still won't get anyone to lay down those
hands for the first raise.

2. The tendencies of the big blind. You should be much
more inclined to steal from a tight big blind. Players who
are trying to survive as long as they can and not get involved
in big pots, players who will not reraise without a premium
hand, players who have no problem being bullied—these
are the players to go after. Usually, they'll just fold and you'll
win the pot. If they decide to play, you can be pretty sure
you're smashed, and you can get away from your hand
cheaply. On the other hand, if you choose to raise a loose
player's big blind, be prepared to play back at him or play a

flop against him if you can't get him to lay down his hand preflop.

In good position, against a tight player's big blind, you can open-raise with any two cards. Under the gun, against a loose player's big blind, you need a premium hand to enter the pot. If the first two factors don't make your decision clear-cut, here are some others to consider.

3. Your hand. Obviously, you're always better off stealing with a hand that has a little something going for it than you are stealing with, say, 7-2o. You want to have the potential to make something just in case you get called. I'd much rather steal-raise with 8-7s than Q-4o. While queen-high will beat 8-7s in a showdown more often than not, 8-7s is a far better hand to open with because you can get aggressive with it on a lot of flops—straight draws, flush draws, and sometimes even one pair. With Q-4o, it's tough to feel comfortable raising on almost any flop.

4. Your opponent's stack size. It's a lot easier to raise with something like K-7o if you know your opponent has to go all-in to call you. You don't want to play a flop with this hand, but you don't mind taking it to a showdown. If your raise puts an opponent to a decision for all his chips, you know that in your worst-case scenario you will have a chance to win the hand in a showdown. Because of this, the more short-stacked your opponent is, the more liberally you can go after his blind.

5. Your image. If you haven't raised a pot in an hour, you're much more likely to get away with a steal-raise than if you've been raising every other hand. When consideration of all the other factors leaves you with a borderline decision, ask yourself what the other players are expecting you to do with the hand. Then do the opposite.

Playing Against a Raise

OK, so you're raising a lot of blinds, winning a lot of pots, and you're not necessarily giving up when you're called. (I'll talk more about this later, but just because my steal-raise gets called doesn't mean the hand is over. I still have the chance to use my postflop skill and find a way to make money on the hand.) The next question is, what do you do when someone raises your blind—or worse, reraises you when you were trying to steal?

There is no simple answer to this question, but if there were it would be something like "you can't just fold every time." A lot of hands are stronger than you might think against a possible steal-raise, or steal-reraise. K-Q, 6-6, J-10, are all hands you should consider defending with against a possible thief. Notice that even though you can sometimes get away with raising hands like K-7o or 9-8o, you probably wouldn't defend with these hands. It takes a stronger hand to call a raise than it does to raise. This is something to keep in mind when your steal-raise gets called by someone other than the big blind. This caller rates to have a strong hand, and you should remember that as you're playing the flop against him.

There are several ways you can go about defending against a steal-raise. You can defend the traditional way, by reraising preflop. But I sometimes like to defend my big blind, and my raises, by calling my opponent's steal-raise and taking a flop. If I hit any pair or draw, I'm liable to get very aggressive and try to take the pot right then and there. Remember, I'm not worried about conserving my chips, or trying to survive as long as possible. I want to be a force at the table. I want my opponents to be afraid to play pots with me.

I might call a steal-raise with 9-8s, then check-raise all-in when I flop a flush draw. I might reraise a stealer with nothing, just knowing he's going to fold a huge chunk of the time. I might even slow-play a big hand against a steal-raise, because I'm calling with enough medium-strength hands that I won't be giving anything away. The point is, I'm never giving up just because someone raised my blind, or reraised me. I'm always looking for any play I can find to pick up chips.

Putting It All Together

I think I've given you a pretty clear idea about when I might steal-raise, or defend against a steal-raise preflop. Let's look at a couple hands from actual World Poker Tour events where these ideas come into play.

On Day Two of the 2004 WPT Championship, two professionals got involved in the following hand. Pro 1, a player with a relatively solid image, raised from early position. Pro 2, a player with a loose-aggressive image, defended his big blind by calling. The flop came down Q-8-5. Pro 2 checked, and Pro 1 bet about half the size of the pot. Pro 2 held 10-9o in his hand, and decided to check-raise. I think he felt Pro 1 would fold a lot of hands in this position, maybe even a hand as strong as J-J, and if he got called he had his gutshot straight draw outs to fall back on. Pro 1, however, held a set of eights and wasn't going anywhere. She reraised a significant amount, putting a little less than half her stack into the pot. This was where it got interesting. Pro 2 moved all-in. Pro 1 called instantly, but Pro 2 hit a runner-runner 6-7 to scoop the pot and eliminate Pro 1.

To many people, Pro 2's play looked wild and even amateurish. No doubt his play was highly aggressive, but I can understand why he did it. First of all, he knew Pro 1 was a tight player, especially since he had just seen her make a big fold about 20 minutes earlier. It was possible, therefore, that Pro 1 would fold anything but a set (and she might have even folded bottom set) to Pro 2's all-in. Since the odds were against Pro 1 holding a set, he stood to win the pot with his all-in raise an enormous chunk of the time. Second, it's not as though Pro 2 had *nothing*. A gutshot straight draw, while not a big hand, or even a big draw, at least gave Pro 2 some hope of winning the pot if he got called. Pro 2's all-in would've been completely unjustifiable with, say, 7-2. But with 10-9, he knew for sure he wasn't drawing dead. Sometimes, that knowledge is the difference between a good play and a terrible play. Third, Pro 2 probably wanted everyone at the table to know that if we raised his blind, we were risking our entire stacks. Sometimes it's not enough to defend your blind by calling preflop, and check-raising the flop as a semi-bluff. Sometimes you just have to follow through with an all-in. Fourth and finally, Pro 2 had about three times as many chips as Pro 1. He could afford to test her, and find out if she really wanted to put her entire tournament life on the line.

I might not have moved in from Pro 2's seat, but then again I might have. It would've depended on my read on Pro 1, and whether I wanted a maniacal image at that particular time at that particular table. But I certainly think Pro 2's play was reasonable, and to this day he's not a player I look to get involved with.

This next hand was played by Matt, but I think it is another good example for instructional purposes. With blinds of $300 and $600 and an ante of $75, Matt raised to $2,000 in late position with A-10o. To Matt's immediate left sat a highly successful, highly aggressive tournament pro who reraised to $6,500. Matt had about $62,000 left, and the pro had him covered. What would you do in Matt's spot?

Matt decided to raise again, making it $20,000 total. The pro thought for a long while, and finally mucked his hand. "Maybe you have me, maybe you don't," the pro said. I like Matt's play on this hand. The pro is well known for coming over the top of his opponents, and Matt had a significantly better-than-average hand for a stealer. Furthermore, Matt didn't want to play a pot out-of-position against a highly skilled opponent. So Matt chose to play back before the flop. It makes sense to me, and obviously it worked out that time.

Raising Preflop to Steal the Blinds

I get asked all the time, "Erick, what happens when I raise preflop trying to steal the blinds, and someone calls me? Do I bet again on the flop? Do I never bet on the flop? Please help!" It's understandable that I get asked these questions so much, because they are very hard to answer. If you bet the flop every time after you raise, your opponent will eventually trap you. If you check the flop every time you miss, you'll get run over with your weak hands, and you'll never get paid with your good hands. So you have to find a happy medium.

Start by asking yourself what kind of hands usually call a pre-flop raise. In my experience, most players that cold-call raises pre-flop have a medium pair, or a small pair, or suited connectors. They don't usually have a big ace or a big pair, and they don't usually have two big cards. OK then, using that logic, you should pretty much bet ace-high flops whether you have the ace or not. After all, you're going to have the ace pretty often, and even when you don't your opponent probably won't have one either. Similarly, flops with two or more big cards are going to be scary to a lot of your opponents' hands, like medium pairs and suited connectors. So those are good flops to fire bets at as well. On the other hand, flops with three low cards are trouble. A lot of times these flops will give your opponent an overpair, or worse, a set. And even if he just has overcards, he may decide to raise, putting you in a tough spot. You should tread lightly on seven-high or eight-high flops. Those flops are the ones where you should probably just check and fold, if you've missed. If you hit those little flops, however, you stand a good chance of getting paid off.

Getting Called on the Flop

If you do follow through with your preflop raise by betting the flop and you get called again, you'll be faced with yet another difficult decision on the turn. This is where your read on your opponent becomes important—possibly more important than the cards on board. Ask yourself, "Why did my opponent call me on the flop?" If the answer is "He has a mediocre hand and he just wants to see if I'll fire another bullet," then you should fire another bullet by betting the turn. Use the same criteria for sizing your bet as you did on the flop (bet larger on boards with many draws; smaller on ragged, rainbow boards). If your opponent is the type who would only call on the flop when slow-playing a monster, then obviously you should shut down. If your read is unclear, you should usually stop betting by the time the turn card comes. Usually, if you've raised preflop and bet the flop and you still haven't lost your opponent, he's in for the long haul in No Limit Hold 'Em. One time this might not be true is when a scare card hits. A lot of players raise their draws in No Limit Hold 'Em. So if a player just calls you on the flop, and the turn card brings the third of a suit, there's a decent chance he will let go of his hand. Of course, it helps to know your player. Some players *always* call with their flush draws, so against them you would probably shut down when the flush card hits. Be sure to look for tells. Most of the time, a player who looks back at his hand when the flush card hits has at most one of the suit. Unless he's a professional giving a reverse tell, he almost never has a flush.

The flush card is the most obvious scare card that can show up on the turn, but there are others that also work to your advantage. If you raise preflop and get called, and then bet the flop and get called, the best card that can show up for you on the turn is an ace. A lot of times that ace will put you into the lead, but even when it doesn't your opponent will have to fear that it does. Just as you should often bet ace-high flops regardless of whether you hold an ace, you should often fire a second bullet when the turn is an ace, whether you have one or not. Having said that, once in a while you should tread lightly when you actually hit the ace. If you suspect your opponent was calling you down with top pair, quite possibly with an ace kicker, it might not be a bad move to go into check-call mode. But again, you have to bet at least sometimes when the ace pairs your hand, or else your opponents will eventually figure out that whenever you bet an ace on the turn, you are bluffing. Everything I just said is somewhat true when a king hits the turn as well. That's because the first hand every poker player puts the raiser on is ace-king.

After you win one of these pots that you've fought hard for and earned with a tough bet or a tough call, you'll look up and realize, "Wow, I'm almost in the money." That's about the time when play in the tournament shifts dramatically. Money scares people. For some reason, even the prospect of winning money scares people. You must not get caught up in the money. You have to keep playing poker, and taking advantage of everyone else's fear.

CHAPTER SIX

Making the Money

This is it. It's late in Day Two, or maybe early in Day Three, of our World Poker Tour event, and you're just a few players away from the money. Now is the moment when you'll either be making nothing or celebrating a five-figure payday.

As tempting as it might be to crawl into a shell and cling to your chips until you lock in your score, that's not the way to play poker tournaments. Even if the lowest payout is a lot of money to you, you have to pretend it isn't. Because the guy who sneaks into the money usually earns about 1 percent of what the winner earns.

Allen Krell, Chris Bigler, Daniel Negreanu, Erick, Dennis Waterman, and Asher Derei: Professional Poker Tour, Commerce.

Don't Play for the Bubble

The fact is that anyone who plays overly conservative at bubble time is costing himself thousands and thousands of dollars in the long run. It is your job to take advantage of these conservative players. The guy who constantly announces how many players are left is the guy whose blind you go after. The guy who talks about how he would only play aces or kings at this stage is the guy to go after. The guy who half-jokes about how he should take a nap in his hotel room until the bubble period ends is the guy to go after. These people will buy you a new car if you just let them. I hear people all the time talk about how "Phil Ivey is raising every hand—not most of the hands, not a lot of the hands, every hand!!" The one thing I never hear is that Phil Ivey went broke playing this way. If the table is going to fold often enough, Phil is going to raise every hand. I will, too, for that matter, if I know my opponents will only play back with aces or kings. Rest assured, if you hear that Phil Ivey is raising every hand, he's not doing it because he's gone crazy. He's doing it because his opponents are playing too tight, and he wants to take maximum advantage.

The hour or so before the bubble is when typical tournament players make the mistake of playing way too tight, and this is often when the stories of Phil Ivey raising every hand start to get passed around from table to table. I'm amazed by how many times I get into the money with fewer chips than I hoped, only to watch 10 or 20 people bust immediately because they were clinging to microstacks for the previous hour. If I squeak into the money and then bust, it's usually because I lost a big pot on the bubble and accidentally snuck into the money because another player went broke. When I get into the money, I almost always get there with chips. You should, too.

When the tournament is exactly one player away from the money, play stops and tables go hand-for-hand. This means that every table starts a hand at the same time, and they wait for all other tables to finish before starting a new hand. If two people bust at the same hand, but on different tables, they both receive the same amount of money no matter who busted "first." This is the *bubble*. And this is a great time to gather chips. Phil Hellmuth is a master at stealing blinds while everyone else is just trying to make it into the money round.

Here is a hand that Matt played at bubble time of a big buy-in tournament. There were 19 players left and only 18 were getting paid, but 18th place was worth more than $10,000. One player had been loud in his agitation over so many hands being played at the bubble. He was just dying to lock in his five-figure score. Matt looked down at K-Jo and opened for a standard raise. It folded to the agitated player, who emphatically slammed a reraise into the pot, putting in about a quarter of his stack. Matt knew this player didn't have a huge hand. First of all, if Agitated Player had a huge hand, he probably would've moved in and not risked busting with it. Second, Matt could tell from Agitated Player's overly aggressive mannerisms that he was probably not crazy about his holding. Matt figured him for jacks or A-K, or possibly queens. Knowing there was a good shot his opponent would fold any of these hands, Matt decided to set Agitated Player all-in. This required Matt to put in about half of his own stack, but he thought it was well worth it. Agitated Player went into a deep think. After a minute had gone by, the table was crowded by railbirds wanting to watch the high-stakes action. Two minutes went by, and Matt heard people mumbling things like "must be kings against aces." After three solid minutes, Agitated Player called and turned over two queens. The crowd was flabbergasted when Matt turned over his K-J. "He likes to gamble," one of the railbirds said. Although Matt does like to gamble, that's not why he made the play. And just because Agitated Player called doesn't make Matt's play bad. Obviously, Agitated Player gave serious thought to folding—and not only that, Matt still had a decent chance to win even after Agitated Player called. Unfortunately for Matt, the queens held up.

In-the-Money Strategy

Finally, the moment approaches. The tournament director announces that a player has been eliminated, the hand-for-hand period is over, and all remaining players are in the money! People will be congratulating themselves, congratulating others at the table, maybe even calling their family members. You'll be congratulating yourself, too—on all the chips you just stole while everyone else played the waiting game.

When the poker gets started again, you'll see players moving their chips. No more waiting around for the short stacks; instead, they'll desperately try to run their piddling chips up to a respectable size. After all, this was their plan—to survive all the way to the money and then hope to get really lucky and somehow win the event. I like to think I don't have to get all that lucky to win a poker tournament (although luck certainly helps, a lot). Still, now is not the time to steal. People will be reckless, and you only want to take them on with some kind of hand. At the same time, you shouldn't wait for aces. Because everyone else is gambling, now might be a good time to take a shot with A-10, or pocket sixes, or even K-Js. You could easily be a favorite over some of the junk people bizarrely take their last stands with. This, of course, assumes that you have chips you can afford to lose in these confrontations.

Usually, all you have to do is catch one good hand to vault up in the chip standings with three or four tables left, snapping off one or more of the short stacks on your way. But what do you do if you somehow become a short stack yourself? As I mentioned in earlier chapters, I don't like to move all-in preflop except as a last resort. But when you have fewer than 10 big blinds and every pot has antes in it to boot, you have reached your last resort. It's time to either move in or fold, and pretty much never do anything else.

The later your position, the more hands you can move in with—and you *don't* want to wait until you only have one or two big blinds in your stack to start moving in. In fact, if it's folded to me when I have only four or five big blinds left, and a tight player is on the big blind, I'm capable of moving in with any two cards. I have a good chance of picking up the blinds and antes, which will increase my stack size about 50 percent! And even if I get called, I always have a shot to win the showdown. That's the thing about moving in with a small stack—it's almost never *that* bad of a play, especially against a tight blind. From an EV standpoint, if you can increase your stack size by 50 percent, and your steal works two out of three times, it's a good play even if you *never* win when you get called. And, of course, you will sometimes win when you get called. Heck, sometimes you'll even have a good hand to start with!

The alternative of waiting for a monster hand will usually leave you with almost no chips. You might have one or two blinds left when you finally find your aces. And guess what happens even if those aces hold up? You're right back where you started, with about four or five big blinds. Waiting for a big hand when you're short will not get you back in the tournament. Aggressively trying to rebuild your stack with somewhat respectable hands (A-x, small pairs, connectors, etc.) is the way to find yourself back in contention for the million-dollar first prize.

Another side of the all-in occurs when one of my opponents moves all-in and it's folded to me in the big blind. Let's assume that in this situation I have chips (I spend very little time as a short stack—I usually either have chips, or I'm out). I call my opponents' all-in raises more frequently than most players would. There are a few reasons for this. First, I don't want to be known as one of the tight players whose blind should be attacked. As I've said before, I want people to be afraid to play a pot with me. Anytime anyone takes an aggressive action toward me, they have to be worried that I'm going to play. Second, once we're in the money, it always helps at least a little to knock players out. If I have the chips to gamble with, I'll do my part to try to move up on the pay scale. (Third, calling is the correct play a lot more often than people think.) And this is the reason to call for calling.

Let's look at a concrete example. The blinds are $3,000–

$6,000 with a $500 ante and I've got $100,000 in chips. A short stack moves in from middle position for $20,000 and everyone folds to me in the big blind. I look down at 8-7s. Many players would just say, "Well, I think he can beat eight-high," and muck their hands. I don't look at it that way. The way I see it, 8-7s is not that far behind a lot of the hands my opponent could have. If he has A-K, or any two big cards, I'm about a 3-to-2 underdog. If he has a small pair, I'm 50-50. Once in a while he'll have a big pair and have me crushed. But look how much money is in the pot—$9,000 from the blinds, $4,500 from the antes, and $20,000 from this player's raise. That's $33,500. And I only have to call $14,000! If I win one time in three, I have more chips than I started the hand with (after posting) in the long run. I should win way more than one time in three, because of all the favorable matchup possibilities I just described. In my view, 8-7s is a no-brainer call in this situation. Not only would I call with 8-7s here, I'd call with J-8o, K-5o, 5-4s, and, of course, hands like pocket deuces and ace-rag. I'm getting a monster price, and I can afford to gamble. In fact, it would be a huge mistake *not* to gamble. Remember, there is luck in this game, but the trick is to know when to try to get lucky. This is one of those times I will try to get lucky.

At this stage of the tournament, you can look fondly back at the time a few hours earlier when you suddenly realized, "Wow, I'm only a few spots from the money." You *can* do that, but you'll probably be too engrossed in the poker to give yourself that luxury. Let me tell you about the revelation that's coming next. It will happen when you ask the tournament director, "Hey, how come we're playing 6-handed over here?" And the director will respond with "Well, there are only 12 players left in the tournament." That's when you'll realize, *"three more players bust, and I'm at the final table."*

With 9 players (or sometimes 10) left in the tournament, the last two tables are combined to one. As you probably know, the World Poker Tour TV broadcast doesn't begin until only 6 players remain. But the poker played from the time 12 players remain until the "TV final table" is reached almost always determines who gets on TV as the chip leader, and who gets on TV as the short stack (and, of course, who doesn't get on TV at all).

Staying Aggressive

Everyone wants to be on TV. Think, however, of how many times you've heard Mike Sexton introduce one of the players as being "on the short stack." How many times have you seen that player win, or even make the top three? The player on the short stack is almost always the first or second one eliminated from the final table. It's true that these players often create marketing opportunities for themselves simply by appearing on television—but do they create a million dollars worth of marketing opportunities? It's a crucial question, because the difference in prize money between first place and sixth place is usually a million dollars or more on the WPT these days.

You can guess where I'm going with this examination of the prize structure. Even with 12 players left—even when you're 3 players away from the final table and 6 players away from the TV final table—you can't play to survive. The prize structure dictates that you play to win. And if you think there are marketing opportunities from appearing on television, just wait and see what the world throws at you when you win one of these things (let alone two). I'm trying to teach you to become a champion—and champions don't limp their way into the final table.

I keep up my aggressive approach when there are 12 players left. Perhaps I'm even more aggressive at this stage, since we're all playing shorthanded and a lot of people are indeed just hoping

they get to appear on TV. There is one exception to this, and that
is if I'm big stack and I'm facing another big stack. Don't get me
wrong—if I have an opportunity to double up at this stage, I'll do
everything I can to take it. But I'm not looking to get involved
with another big stack. It's just so much easier to go after the
short stacks who are clinging to their chips hoping to survive. Big
stacks are usually big stacks for a reason—either they're good
players who have earned their chips, loose/aggressive players
who've gotten lucky, or both. I'm not trying to tangle with a
loose player or a good player at this stage of the game. I'm trying
to attack the weak-tight guys who are just happy to have made it
so far.

Playing Conservative Against the Big Stack

Let's look at a hand example that would play very differently
against a big stack than it would against a small or medium stack.
I'm in middle position and open for a raise with A-9. A smallish
stack calls me on the button. He's only got about the size of the
current pot in his stack after he calls my raise. I'm first to act on
the flop and it comes ace-high. I'm putting my opponent all-in.
Either I'm going to move in myself, or I'm going to check
with the intention of calling my opponent's all-in. The point
is, this guy is not "winning" this hand without putting all
his chips in the pot. Even if I don't flop an ace, I'm going to set
my opponent all-in a good chunk of the time—pretty much
anytime big cards flop or I think the board just missed him.
Now, let's say instead that a big stack called my raise on the button. If the flop comes ace-high, I may well check and fold! If I
don't check, but instead decide to bet, I'm almost certainly folding to a raise. If I check and call, I probably won't check and call
a second time.

Why would I play so conservatively against the big stack? Well, first of all, I don't really have a hand. Top pair with a nine kicker is a monster against a short stack, but it's a piece of junk when both players have a lot of chips. Second, I'm out of position. I don't want to put myself into difficult decisions out of position when I can simply fold and go back to hammering away at the short stacks on the very next hand. Finally, the big stack probably has a hand if he's calling me. Most big stacks don't want to risk elimination in the tournament by running into another big stack, and while I'll gladly risk elimination if it means increasing my chances to win the event, not everyone plays like I do. When you get down to it, no one likes to go broke—not even me. But if you can make everyone else believe you don't care about risking all your chips, you have an enormous advantage. That's what happens when another big stack enters a pot with me: he's telling me he'll risk going broke with this hand. And that usually means I have to get out of the way.

With every player that gets eliminated, the desire to reach the final six of a WPT event no matter the cost becomes more and more noticeable among the remaining contestants. You must try to fight this desire yourself. Keep winning in mind. Imagine yourself standing next to Mike Sexton, beer in hand, the toast of the poker world. That's your aim. Your aim is not to make the final six and ensure that the producers strap the microphone to your back, get you all made-up, and force you to put your hole cards in exactly the right spot. Your aim is to win. Convince yourself that everything else is an obstacle to that objective, because in a way, everything else is.

Even with seven players left—especially with seven players left—you can't be thinking about the TV cameras. If you play to win with seven players left, you may just find yourself a champion a day later.

With seven players left in the 2004 World Poker Tour Championship, Matt was fourth in chips when his opponent moved all-in on the river for $1.3 million in chips. There was only $900,000 in the pot, meaning Matt's opponent probably had a very big hand, or absolutely nothing. The river had brought a third diamond, and Matt's opponent's bet was saying, "I have a flush; get out." Matt had a straight. I think many players would've quietly folded rather than risk $1.3 million on this call. Matt only had $1.6 million left himself, and would've been a near lock for seventh if he called and was wrong. The problem was, Matt didn't think his opponent had the flush. Based on the way his opponent had played his hand up to that point, Matt felt confident his straight was good. He felt confident enough to call a $1.3 million all-in. And Matt was right. His opponent was on a stone bluff, and Matt entered the final table second in chips. He ended up finishing third, but instead of winning $100,000 or $200,000 for sixth or seventh (his likely finish if he'd folded), Matt won $700,000 for third. Not only that, he put himself in great position to win the title. It doesn't always work out, of course, but third is still much, much better than seventh, or sixth.

But trust me, finishing third or fourth or fifth is just as heartbreaking as finishing seventh. If I don't give myself a chance to win the event, I have trouble sleeping at night. As unhealthy as that may be, I think all good players are perfectionists like this in one way or another.

After what might have been hours and hours of poker, finally, a player busts out in seventh place. Maybe you busted him, maybe you didn't. It doesn't really matter, because you're going to the TV final table! You can celebrate now, because you have the rest of the night off. But the next day will be the biggest of your poker career.

CHAPTER SEVEN

The Final Table

Everyone always says, "See you at the final table." Only six players in a World Poker Tour event actually make it to the last day—a day of interviews, waiting, maybe some shopping for new TV-worthy clothes, and, finally, poker. It's an experience you'll remember when you're wrinkled, and you want to remember it with a smile. So play your very best poker. If you don't win, you'll at least be able to say you held nothing back. Leave everything on the table.

There is nothing you can do as a poker player to fully prepare for a WPT final table. The crowd surrounds the venue, the lights

Dan Heimiller, Lee Markholt, Barry Shulman, Chris Bjorin, Erick, and Doyle Brunson: Professional Poker Tour, Bellagio

are hot, and the stakes are huge. You won't truly be ready for it until you've experienced it yourself. But you can put yourself in a better position than your opponents.

Focus

My first piece of advice is to *focus*. This will also be my last piece of advice (don't worry, I'll have some other stuff in the middle). The fact is, you're not going to become a significantly better poker player from the time the tournament starts to the time it ends. You'll play pretty much the same game at the final table that got you to the final table. The one thing you *can* do, however, is avoid the distractions by focusing on the poker, and only on the poker. The tournament director will constantly be talking on the microphone, Mike Sexton and Vince Van Patten

will be jabbering away in the background, Shana Hiatt or Court-
ney Friel will be walking around filming sound bites, and there
will be a pile of cash waiting not far from the table. Ignore all of
it. Play poker. Do that, and you'll be at least a step ahead of the
competition.

When It's Right to Slide Up the Pay Scale

Now, there are some important things about the actual poker
contest you should keep in mind at the final table. I've been saying throughout the book that you have to play to win. *Play to win,
not to survive; play to win, not to survive.* It's been my mantra. But at
the final table, especially when it gets down to three or four players, there are exceptions to my mantra. The difference between
second place and third place, and between third place and fourth
place, is significant. With 100 people left, it doesn't make sense to
make sure you get to the top 50, because there is almost no reward for doing so. With four players left, it *does* sometimes make
sense to fold a few hands to make sure you get into the top three.
This is particularly true if one or two players have short stacks
and a big stack has raised. You stand a very good chance of finishing second or third, if not first, by folding. If you play against the
stack, you risk finishing fourth and earning significantly less
money. Therefore, unless you're playing in a tournament where
first place is much, much higher than second, it requires a very
big hand to confront a big stack at the final table, assuming you
have a big stack yourself. Of course, if you're a short stack, you
should do everything you can to get chips. You won't be able to
sit back and hope someone with more chips goes bust.

The flip side of this is that you can make the first raise with
any two cards. Busting at this stage of the game can be so costly
that your opponents are not likely to call you without a big hand.

But the blinds and antes will be at their biggest. These facts add up to a blind stealer's paradise. Ever wonder why you see so many WPT final table players, like Gus Hansen and Tuan Le, raising with junk hands like 7-3 and 2-4? This is why.

The First Player to Enter the Pot
Controls the Hand

At final tables, even more so than in other situations, the first player to enter the pot controls the hand. You can open-raise with more hands at a final table than at any other time in the tournament, but you can't call raises, or even reraise yourself, as often as you can earlier on.

I remember my first WPT final table like it was yesterday. It was July 2003 in the high-class Aviation Club in Paris, France. I always find it a little harder to play my best poker when I have to travel to a tournament, and Paris is farther from Vegas than any other city on the WPT schedule. Sleep was hard to come by, and the long hours we played to reach the final table were wearing on me. Even though I was exhausted, as soon as the cards went in the air that last time, I suddenly sprung to life.

In the very first hand, Lee Salem opened the pot for a raise under the gun. I looked down to see the ace-jack of hearts. With David Benyamine and Jan Boubli to my left, two very aggressive and tough French players, I was in a tough spot. Also, Lee Salem is not the type to get overly tricky. When he opens the pot under the gun, he generally has a hand. After some deliberation, I folded my suited A-J—a hand that normally has a ton of value in a six-handed game.

Early in my poker career, I would often make a play because I thought I had to, or because I thought to myself, "A pro would definitely raise here, he would never pass on this strong of a hand." I have since learned that if I'm not comfortable reraising, folding or calling are perfectly valid alternatives. And A-J in particular is a hand with which I usually like to reraise or fold. Given what I knew about the players, I like my fold in this spot.

On the WPT broadcast, Mike Sexton and Vince Van Patten seemed shocked that I folded the hand. I guess they learned for the first time that my loose-aggressive image is often just an image. I was sick when I watched the telecast and learned that Lee Salem held Q-Js, in my opinion about the worst hand he'd enter the pot with from that seat. But I was then very relieved to see that Jan Boubli had A-Q behind me. If I had chosen to reraise with my A-Js, I might very well have committed all my chips with it against an aggressive player like Jan. This hand set the tone for the rest of the table, where I am proud of many other decisions I made.

David Benyamine was the man to beat at this table. He'd been on a roll the night before, a roll that carried him through to the last hand of the night, when he busted Daniel Negreanu in seventh place. Nothing had changed a day later, and David was still rolling. I knew he wanted to pick on the others, but I knew he didn't really want to pick on me, even though he had position. Similarly, I was trying to avoid him for the time being, and hoping our confrontation would come during the heads-up portion of events. Sometimes, however, the best-laid plans fall apart in front of us. The following was probably the toughest hand I ever played.

I was in the small blind with 10-7s and chose to call the extra $2,000. David checked his option, so we saw the flop heads-up. It came 10-9-6, and I decided to lead out for $8,000. David raised me quickly to $28,000. I read strength on David immediately, but there was no way I was folding. Top pair with a gut-shot straight draw is a huge hand in a blind-on-blind situation. In other words,

I knew David was strong, but I was strong, too. I needed more information before proceeding. So I called. The turn came an off-suit five and I checked, again looking for information. David reached for his chips but pulled back. After some deliberation he said, "Sixty, good number," meaning he was betting $60,000—almost the size of the pot. I decided it was time to chat. "What you got, David?" I said. And he started talking and talking and talking. At one point, he even said that he was afraid I had limped in with an overpair to trap him. David talked as much as any opponent I've ever faced. Was he talking now because he was bluffing or because he was strong? I thought his bet was pretty large, and I wondered if he had a hand like a pair and straight draw. It felt like he was scared to let me see a river. I thought David would've raised preflop with J-10 or better, so I ruled out top pair with a better kicker. So the question became "Does he have two pair or the straight?" I knew he would bet less than $60,000 with a straight, to milk me for more chips. All of this thinking was done in about a minute, at the most important and pressure-packed table I had ever played. I decided he had 6-5 in his hand for bottom two pair. *Great,* I thought, *I know he has me beat, so I will fold.* The bad news was the pot was laying me a decent price to play if he indeed held 6-5. In fact, there was $66,500 in the pot before David's bet. The pot was laying me more than 2 to 1. I was nearly certain an 8 would win me the pot, and I liked my chances if a 10 or a 7 came. In the end, however, I decided I didn't have enough outs to call against David's almost certain two pair. So I folded.

David looked visibly startled when I mucked. He gathered himself and said he could show me a three. "If you show me a three," I replied, "I'll fall out of my chair." David mucked his hand facedown, and I had to wait for the WPT broadcast to see that he had 10-6 for two pair. My hand was nearly a 4-to-1 underdog. When I watch this hand being replayed on the WPT Season 2

DVD, I am very proud that I took my time and was as calculating as I am now recounting the hand. It was probably one of the biggest laydowns you will see on the WPT, and definitely one of the best, if I do say so myself!

The game continued on, and although David was in control, the rest of the players at the final table were no bargain. The tightest guy at the table was probably George the Greek. I had trouble taking advantage of this, however, because I was directly to his left. So when George had the big blind, I was under the gun. Once the blinds went up to $4,000-$8,000, I knew I only had a round or two left to make a move. I looked down at 8-6o under the gun and decided to raise all-in to $57,000. At the time, my thought process was that I had to pick on George's blind. I wasn't entirely comfortable moving in, but I had one of those difficult stack sizes that I discussed earlier. Any raise less than an all-in would've left me very close to pot-committed. If I had made a minimum raise to $16,000, I would've been able to fold to a reraise, but the minimum raise offers my opponents quite a price to call—and this was obviously a situation where I didn't want anyone to call. And, of course, I could've folded the hand outright and taken my chances with seven big blinds in my stack. At the time, however, I didn't think through those options carefully enough. I didn't get past my first thought—that I should go after George's blind. I learned a valuable lesson about finding ways to play poker to the end. I no longer think moving in was my best choice in this hand. After all, who is to say I wouldn't have found a real hand and doubled up on the very next deal? Poker is a game of short-term luck and long-term skill. I didn't give myself enough of a chance to get lucky with this play, as 8-6o is just too often in bad shape when it gets called. It was a hard lesson to swallow when I realized I had left $340,000 and my dream of a WPT title on the table. The silver lining was that I carried the lessons I learned in Paris with me to the next WPT event—in sunny Aruba.

We had 436 people enter the 2003 Ultimate Poker Classic in Aruba. Although fields that size are common these days, back then it was pretty large. As a result, the blinds had to go up very quickly late in the tournament so that we got down to 6 players at a reasonable hour. To comply with the WPT final table structure requirements, we actually had to roll back the blinds two levels for the final day's play. This meant the poker we played the night before was different from what we faced for the television cameras. The night before, the players seemed timid and scared trying to make it on TV. Boy, did things change once their stacks got deeper. These guys were wild gamblers. Anthony Fagan and Daniel Larsson came out firing, and I was not nearly ready for the bluffs they made early on. When you're at the final table, be observant immediately of how players have changed from the night before, as sometimes those changes can be drastic.

As I said earlier, when I travel I tend to be tired, and the Aruba tournament was no exception. Although I thought I was the best player at the table, I knew I didn't have my A game. This meant I had to look to catch some breaks. If you have seen the show, you know that I caught more than a few breaks—namely, three pairs of pocket aces! I first got them early on, when Anthony had already established his aggressive style of play. He raised to $50,000 with what turned out to be K-J, while I was in the big blind. I decided to reraise to $150,000, giving him some rope to hang himself. By making the standard reraise he would expect from me, I thought I might be able to induce him to move all-in, or at least call my raise. This is a straightforward play, but the interesting decision came after he called and we took a flop. The flop came 3-6-7, and I decided to go all-in, hoping he had pocket eights or better. Since he called my raise before the flop, I figured him for a decent hand like two jacks, so this seemed like a good spot to put my chips in. In retrospect, I really could have checked to him and hoped he made a mistake. Unfortunately, because I moved in, he was able to get away. By being aggressive, I often get my opponents to call me with bad hands, but sometimes even I fail to get action. After all, if my bets got called every time, bluffing would become an ineffective strategy for me really fast. Once in a while, though, even I have to consider slow-playing to get paid.

Daniel Larsson was another player who had undergone an overnight transformation. He had played very conservatively the previous day, but the final table brought a new Daniel. He raised to $30,000 on the button and I called him in the small blind with K-9, thinking I could outplay him on the later streets. The flop came A-9-3 and I checked. Daniel bet $30,000 and I called. The turn was a blank, and I then decided to lead out for $60,000 into the $144,000 pot to get a better read. He made it $160,000 pretty quickly. I had made what I call a weak lead—an out-of-position bet of about 40 percent of the pot. I should've expected to get raised. So often the weak lead is made by a player with a marginal hand trying to figure out where he is at, and that was exactly what I had done here. If I had checked to Daniel, he may have checked behind me, or I could've elected to check-call. By throwing the $60,000 bet out there, it was almost as if I had told him, "I have a hand, but it's not that good." He made a terrific raise, and even though I suspected that I held the best hand, I chose to fold. I did this largely because of the weakness of the remaining players, but also because I didn't want to face yet another difficult decision on the river. Kudos to Daniel for a great bluff. I had to wait until the show aired on the Travel Channel to find out what he had. It turns out he had K-7, and no outs if I'd decided to play.

The weak lead can be effective if it stuns your opponent into calling a small bet, when a check would've induced a much larger bet (one that you don't want to call). As I mentioned in chapter 4, you might make this play when you're on a draw. The weak lead can also be a great way to trap with a monster. But the weak lead is usually not a very good play with a medium-strength hand like I had unless it's done on the river (refer back to chapter 4). When you're ahead, you usually make the most money by inducing the bluff—and you don't invite the disaster of folding the best hand to a raise with this approach. Checking also allows your opponent to check behind you. Finally, checking puts the action on your opponent, and possibly allows you to pick up a tell on him for free. If you must bet with a medium-strength hand, make a real bet. That at least makes it less likely that you'll get bluff-raised out of the pot. But save your weak leads on the turn for when you have a draw, or the nuts.

Not Everyone Plays By the "Rules"

I think these examples should give you a very good idea of what to do and what not to do at a WPT final table. There is, however, an odd thing about final table poker. Watch the Travel Channel on Wednesday nights and you'll see some very unorthodox plays. Some people see an unorthodox play and assume it was made by an amateur—an unskilled player who fluked his way into the final table. While players do sometimes fluke their way to the final table, you should think twice before deciding that every strange play you see is a bad play. Sometimes it's the creative final table player who gets all the money.

Gus Hansen has won two World Poker Tour events. Only Howard Lederer, Daniel Negreanu, Tuan Le, and I have equaled that feat at the time of this writing. Yet Gus consistently gets involved with junk hands at the final table. There are a couple of reasons he gets away with this. First of all, he's an outstanding postflop player. Throughout the tournament, Gus takes flops against his opponents and learns their tendencies and how to exploit them, just as I do. It's very hard to turn playing styles off and on in an instant. Gus has a lot of practice playing the way he does—he doesn't show up at the final table and just decide to make a lot of unorthodox plays. While watching the WPT on television is a great teaching tool, keep in mind that you don't always see every single hand played. So Gus's unorthodox play may be a result of information he's gathered from hands not aired on television. If you're not used to making a reraise or a call with junk every once in a while, I wouldn't suggest trying these things for the first time at the final table. But if you follow the advice in this book, you'll be involved in a lot of hands and probably pick up some strange plays for your arsenal, if only by default.

Unorthodox play also works at the final table because players are less likely to call for all their chips than at any other time in the tournament. For all the reasons I mentioned earlier, people are not looking to go broke at this stage. Playing junk at other stages of the tournament usually fails because your opponents play back at you too often. But in the right situation at the final table, your opponents might fold often enough to make anything playable. In the first World Poker Tour event that I won, Aruba 2003, my opponents seemed to fold every hand for hours. I sat back, raised selectively, and slowly accumulated chips. It's important to know your opponents at the final table—even more important than it is during the rest of the event. Luckily, you will have been playing with your final table opponents for quite a while before the first TV hand is dealt.

Remember, the top three spots are where the money is, and

the top spot is worth even more than the already sizable first prize. I'm not just talking about the WPT title either (although that's great, too). The *winner* of a WPT final table has a much greater chance to market himself or herself than any of the other final tableists who have simply made it on TV. Final table players are just players. The person who wins is a champion—and that will stay with him or her forever. So when the dust has cleared and there are only two players remaining in your World Poker Tour event, do not become complacent. You may have already won an enormous sum of money, and you may have already put four days of tireless effort into this tournament, but you've got to save the best for last. The most important part of the event remains to be played.

CHAPTER EIGHT

Heads-up Play

It's money time. Heads-up play is what separates the WPT champion from the first loser. I'll show you how to be a champion.

The skill factor in a poker game tends to get bigger and bigger as the number of opponents goes down. So unless you've spent many hours at the final table and the blinds have become absurdly large in relation to the stacks, the heads-up portion of the tournament will require more skill than any stage you've played up to that point. It makes sense, then, that the pay difference between first and second place is bigger than that of any other two places.

Daniel and Erick heads-up

I've been heads-up at the final of two World Poker Tour events, and won them both. I've also been heads-up in many other big tournaments, including a Professional Poker Tour event, which I also won. In addition to those, I've played hundreds of heads-up matches online, many of which had buy-ins of $5,000. So I guess you can say I'm an experienced heads-up player.

Don't Have Any Set Style in Heads-up Play

If I could make one rule about heads-up play, it would be "don't have any rules." Every individual opponent has his own idiosyncrasies, things he'll do or plays he'll make that are unique to him (or her). Observe your opponent carefully and find an effective way to take his chips. If he bluffs too much, let him. If he folds too much, bet just often enough to keep him folding, but not so often that he stops folding. And if he calls too much, give up on your bluffs, but bet the tiniest little made hand—like bottom pair, ace-high, or even king-high—against him.

As you can see, it's very important to use all your weapons as a poker player in a heads-up match. There is time and place for check-calling, check-folding, check-raising, betting out small, betting out big, bluffing, bluff-raising, and even bluff-reraising. Don't go into a heads-up match with a fixed idea of how you're supposed to be playing. Don't make the mistake I used to make early in my career of thinking that "a pro would play this way in a heads-up match, so I'm going to do the same thing he would do." Play your game—which is to say, play your opponent.

Bluffing

Let's go into more detail about some of your weapons in a heads-up match. Take bluffing. Just as you should be observing your opponent, your opponent will be observing you. Therefore, unless you never ever want action on your good hands, you're going to have to bluff sometimes. As I alluded to above, you'll be bluffing more against players who are folding too much, which of course makes sense. But the great thing about No Limit Hold 'Em is you can make it very difficult for your opponents to call with mediocre hands. If my instinct tells me my opponent won't call a big bet, it's bluffing time. And if I had the nuts every time I bet, I would never get paid. I avoid that problem by bluffing. It's fun *and* profitable in a heads-up situation.

Value Betting

Now that you're a bluffer, make sure you're a value bettor, too. If you bluff every time, your opponent is going to figure it out, and he'll just sit back and trap you. Believe me, I know. I've busted a lot of people this way. Don't be afraid to bet your hands. You'll be amazed at how often you'll get called, especially if you play the aggressive style I've been recommending throughout this book. My favorite heads-up opponents are the ones who fold for the small bets, but make "great calls" when I overbet. I love these guys. I can bluff with little risk, and get enormous value from my real hands. Players call off their chips a lot more often in heads-up play than at any other time of the tournament. After all, they're only facing one opponent, they've already locked up second-place money, and their jack-high might even be the best hand! Use that to your advantage by playing your nut hands the same way you play your bluffs.

Sizing Your Bets

Be very careful to size your bets appropriately during heads-up play. The "nuisance" raise I discussed earlier becomes even more powerful heads-up. Preflop, I pretty much always open for double the big blind if I want to raise in a heads-up match. I'm dying to take flops in position, and I don't want to blow my opponent off his hand preflop. Similarly, I make small bets and raises after the flop. I want to keep my opponent off balance. I'm looking to probe for information any way I can. I want my opponent to sometimes fold to my bluffs when I bet small, but still have incentive to call those small bets so I get paid on my monsters.

Check-Call

The most underrated heads-up weapon is also one of the most underrated weapons in poker, period—and that's the check-call. Some players think aggression is the only skill needed in a heads-up match. If you check to these players, don't you worry, they're going to bet. I make a lot of money against players by check-calling against them—on the flop, on the turn, and sometimes even on the river if they're stubborn enough to bet a third time. Think about it. If I bet my small pairs and my opponent always folds, I win a tiny pot. But if I check and call down an opponent who will bet with just about anything, I pick up a lot more money. I get sucked out on a little more often by playing this way, but that's a risk I'm more than willing to take. It's not about winning the pot. It's about winning money.

Know When to Adjust

However you end up playing against your opponent, make sure you don't get locked into a certain style. Heads-up play is largely about adjusting. If your opponent catches on that you're trying to trap him, start bluffing him instead. If your opponent figures out that he's getting run over, sit back and wait for a hand before you bet again. The point is—and it's a point I've repeated throughout this book—that you have to constantly reassess what's going on at the poker table and pick an approach that will work for the current situation. You don't pick an approach that would've worked the night before, or an hour before, or even five minutes before. Always try to be a few steps ahead of your opponent. That's how you win a poker tournament.

Moving All In

Of course, in an ideal world, you'll get to the heads-up portion of the tournament with a nice-sized chip lead. That sure makes things easier, or at least simpler. If one of the players in a heads-up match has 10 big blinds or fewer in front of him, it really becomes a preflop all-in fest. If you're first-to-act, you should shove in with lots of hands—any ace, any king, any suited jack, any pair, some big cards, and some connecting cards. This holds true whether you're the big stack or the small stack. The small stack has to aggressively go after chips, and the big stack has to keep the pressure on the small stack. Similarly, if the other guy moves in on you, you should be inclined to call pretty often. You're not waiting for A-K here. Call with any ace, any pair, most kings, and even hands like Q-9s. You can't allow yourself to get run over, as the big stack, or as the small stack. Your opponent is supposed to be attacking your blind liberally—so you have to defend it liberally as well. This strategy, of course, can and should be changed if your opponent is overly tight, or overly loose. But against a competent opponent, your best bet is usually to attack and defend with quite a few hands, giving yourself a great chance to either double up if you're short, or put the match away if you're ahead.

I followed my own advice on that glorious afternoon in Aruba. I was picking up hand after hand, as anyone who's seen the show can attest to. I caught so many hands I almost had to apologize to the other players at the table! A lot of players could've won with the cards I had. But I put myself in position to get lucky, and that's all we can do in this game. (I really hope you've learned that by chapter 8.)

The blinds had risen to $40,000–$80,000, and I had Daniel Larsson on the ropes. He posted his small blind and decided to call. I thought this was a strange move on his behalf, as it left him with only $375,000. Including antes, there was now $180,000 in the pot as I looked down at Q-3 of diamonds. I knew there was a chance Daniel had limped in with a big hand, but I didn't think he held a huge hand. If I'd been first to act, moving in would've been clear, with Daniel as short-stacked as he was. But his limp got me thinking. I finally decided that if there was any chance he would fold, I needed to move all my chips in. So I did. He called immediately with A–K. I like Daniel's play because he really wanted to double up, and I had been moving in a lot. On the other hand, picking up the sizable pot without risk would have been nice for him as well, since he was only about a 2-to-1 favorite over my hand. Sure enough, I hit a queen on the flop and ended the heads-up match with a three on the turn. My first WPT victory was in the books.

CHAPTER NINE

Living the Life of a Pro

It's a nice feeling, isn't it? Carrying a few million dollars worth of chips to the cage and telling the cashier, "I'd like to wire this home, please. No problem, I'll cover the $10 transfer fee." If you're a typical player, winning a World Poker Tour event will move your bank account from four or five figures to six or seven figures. Man, does that next bank statement look sweet.

What to Do with a Million Dollars

Most people don't actually know what they'd do with a million dollars. They claim they'd buy a nice house, or a nice car, or

Erick with his winning hand and the big check at the PartyPoker Million

make a bunch of great investments. All these things are fine ideas, but after you start looking seriously into any of them, you're going to find out that a million dollars actually isn't as much money as it appears to be. OK, a million dollars is clearly a lot of money, and life-changing money for 99.9 percent of poker players, I'm sure. But it's not nearly enough money so that you can buy anything and everything you'd want. It's not enough money so that you should stop thinking about money. And, especially if you're a gambler, it's not enough money so that you can stay in action for the rest of your life, or even for the next few years, or even for the next week if you decide to jump into the $4,000-$8,000 game at the Bellagio with the likes of Barry Greenstein, Ted Forrest, Doyle Brunson, Gus Hansen, and Phil Ivey.

It's great to win a million dollars, but it's useless if you're not smart about it. Believe me, I know. I've made my fair share of bad bankroll decisions in my career, and I'm trying to prevent my readers from making some of the same mistakes I did. I'm also going to give you some ideas about fun and profitable things you *can* do with your new winnings.

You Have to Pay Your Taxes

First, I have some bad news. Even though you probably won't get any forms or be required to leave your Social Security number behind when you leave town, U.S. law still mandates that you pay income taxes on your winnings. A lot of players wonder if they could just get away with not reporting their tournament winnings. It's one thing to "forget" to report a $20 lottery ticket, or a hundred bucks won in a $10-$20 Hold 'Em game. It's another thing to fail to report a million dollars in gambling income. That's the kind of thing you'd go to jail for if you got caught. If you're OK with that risk, more power to you, but even I'm not *that* much of a gambler. I suggest you set aside 40 percent of your winnings (less if you live in a state with no state income tax, like Nevada) and invest them in some low-risk way, like a Treasury bill or a CD. You might not have to give all of that to the government come tax season, but at least you'll be ready if you do. The good news about paying taxes on a big win is that the government has a piece of your action for the rest of the year. You can and should deduct gambling losses, including and especially tournament buy-ins, from your gambling wins. The tricky (and, in my opinion, unfair) part is that you can't carry a gambling loss over from year to year. If I win a million this year on the tournament circuit, I owe taxes on that million. But if I lose a million next year, there is no tax deduction I can make for it in that or any other year. It is smart, therefore, to play as many events as you can afford after a big win. Once you've won a million dollars, $10,000 events don't really cost $10,000 for the rest of the year.

That's because you get a tax rebate if you lose. The government always gets a piece of your winnings. Only if you win big will the government actually take a chunk of your losses. So let's play poker, baby!

Where Do You Go from Here?

The first decision you need to make (and you should wait until you have a cool head to make it) is what kind of poker you're going to play. My advice is not to jump up more than two limits from your previous regular game. For example, if you are a $3-$6 player who found a way to satellite into a World Poker Tour event and then take it down for a million bucks, I still wouldn't play any bigger than $10-$20 for at least a few months. There is a lot of luck in this game, and while you and I both know that you won the tournament because you skillfully applied all that you learned from this book, it's important to at least concede the possibility that you're not the best poker player in the world just yet. You're going to have plenty of time to work your way into the higher-limit games. Play a few hundred hours at $10-$20, and if you're smashing it, move up to $20-$40. The highest-limit games aren't going anywhere—and a million dollars isn't nearly enough of a bankroll to sit in them. If your goal is to play the big game at Bellagio, make it a long-term goal—really long. I've won two World Poker Tour events, and even I don't sit in that game.

Maybe you were a $15-$30 player who wants to move up to $50-$100. I think that's a reasonable increase, and you've got the bankroll to withstand the swings at that level. The point is, there is more to moving up in limits than having the bankroll. The players are more and more skilled (in general) the higher you go. If you win a WPT event, that's a good indication that you're a significantly better player than what is typical for your usual game. But it doesn't mean you should immediately jump into the biggest game you can find. In fact, doing so would probably be a disaster.

Creating a Bankroll

Once you've picked your new regular poker game, you should set aside a bankroll for that game. If you're going to make poker your career, then I highly advise having a separate bankroll for poker, independent of your investments and your living expenses. You should figure out how much you need to play poker properly. I would recommend no less than 500 big bets if you're playing Limit Hold 'Em. If you prefer the No Limit Hold 'Em ring games, you probably would need 10,000 big blinds to feel comfortable. Once you've picked your bankroll number, you should only extract money from your bankroll if you are in excess of that number.

Make sure when picking your bankroll number that you factor in tournaments. I strongly recommend learning to play both cash games and tournaments well, and as I mentioned above, it will be in your best interest to play a lot of tournaments for the rest of the year for tax reasons. Let's say there are seven or eight World Poker Tour events remaining on the schedule for the calendar year after your big win. If you're going to play them all, you need to factor in travel expenses, satellite buy-ins, and, of course, the actual tournament buy-ins into your bankroll. It adds up quickly, and you may end up deciding that you *don't* want to play every single major tournament for the rest of the year. Or you may decide to look for a backer.

The Life

The life of a traveling poker pro is exhausting, expensive, and I think unique. Can you name another occupation that requires traveling around the world risking tens of thousands of dollars in the hopes of making a big score? Ours is a solitary occupation as well—a lot of time spent alone in hotel rooms and on flights. Even at the table, it's usually a case of Me Against The World, and not always as social a game as it seems. That's why a lot of the top pros become friends away from the table. We're constantly running into each other in cities and casinos where we don't know another soul. So it's only natural that a certain camaraderie develops. To me, if the poker world weren't filled with fun and interesting players that are ready to play some golf, or shoot some pool, or go out partying at any time (with wagering involved in any or all activities), it wouldn't be worth it to play the circuit. If you're going to become a tournament pro, get ready for a whole new social scene.

Of course, if you're going to keep your "real job" and continue to treat poker as an avocation, then bankroll requirements aren't nearly as meaningful. I mean, if you can fully replenish your poker bankroll at any time with money that you earn in the real world, then you can pretty much play any game, so long as you're OK with having a really bad session in it. When you play poker for a living, you have to be able to withstand a lot of bad sessions in a row. Even the best of us go through stretches where we have a lot of bad sessions in a row. But if you can add money to your bankroll more or less at will, then you don't need to worry so much, and you'll probably have a lot more fun playing poker than the pros do. Most pros, especially cash-game pros, treat poker as work. Because for them, it is. If you don't want poker to become your work, you might want to seriously consider keeping your day job—even after you win a million dollars on the WPT.

OK, you've figured out your poker bankroll; now how much money do you have left? If you're going to be a professional poker player, the next thing you need to do is set aside money for living expenses, preferably at least six months' worth. Six months should be enough time, if you play reasonably often, so that the luck will even out and you'll earn enough to withdraw from your bankroll. In the meantime, however, make sure you're never sweating to pay your rent/mortgage, your cell phone bill, your cable bill, your car payment, or whatever other costs you may incur, like travel expenses on the tournament circuit. And oh yeah, don't forget about food. Most poker players like food, and everyone in Vegas knows it. Once again, if you're not playing for a living, you can count on your real job to pay the bills (that's pretty much the entire point of keeping your day job, right?).

Finally, after setting aside all that dough for boring stuff like a poker bankroll and living expenses, you can examine the rest of your winnings and start to have some fun. Put a down payment on a house. That's fun! At least it was for me—I've got a place in Vegas with six plasma TVs and a lighted basketball court. But if that's not your style, you can also buy a whole mess of artwork (although I guess the connoisseur wouldn't call it a "mess"), or a colonial with a front lawn for gardening, or whatever. To me, one of the best things about having money is that you can have a place of your own. No landlords, no condo boards, and no concern about which walls you can or can't knock down. Home ownership is the nuts.

If you live in New York, or Washington, D.C., or San Francisco, or anyplace where the market is ridiculously out of whack, you won't be able to pay cash for a home with your new winnings—not if you want to have any money left over anyway. Unfortunately, the same thing is becoming true in Las Vegas, the fastest-growing real estate market in the country. So rather than pay cash for your new home, you'll probably have to do what "normal" people do—take out a mortgage. If you have a real job, getting a loan will be easy. If you're a poker player, getting a loan will still be easy, but you'll have to pay a higher interest rate.

Wherever you were living when you hit it big on the World Poker Tour, you might want to consider relocating to Las Vegas, Nevada. The most obvious reason to move to Vegas is that most of the big tournaments are there. If you're planning to play the circuit, I'd guess that living in Vegas will cut down on your travel expenses by $10,000 or more per year. But the next reason, one that I mentioned earlier, might be an even bigger motivating factor to make the move. There is no state income tax in Nevada. This fact won't help you get out of paying taxes on the money you've already won (as you're required to report your winnings in the state where you lived *when you won*), but it will lessen the tax burden on any future winnings. On top of everything else, you'll be living in Vegas! If you're a young person who's into going out and having a good time, there is no better city for a professional poker player than Las Vegas. If you're not into those things, then maybe this last point isn't really a selling point for you.

The key to shopping for a home is deciding how much money you should spend on the down payment. At this point, you've already set aside money for taxes, poker bankroll, and living expenses. So based on what you've budgeted for living expenses, figure out what kind of monthly mortgage payment fits into your plan. (You can also reverse-engineer this; i.e., figure out how much you'll be paying each month for your mortgage and *then* allocate your living expenses.) Now you should have a pretty good idea of what's left for a down payment. If you've won a million dollars, you should have at least a couple hundred thousand left over, even after everything else, to put into a house (unless you're *really* living the high life). Investing in real estate is a great way to have fun and make money at the same time—sort of like playing poker with houses instead of chips.

I could try to tell you more about bankroll management, but it really all comes down to one simple sentence: don't blow it. I hear about poker players all the time who flush their winnings down the toilet—players who've won hundreds of thousands of dollars on the circuit who suddenly can't afford a buy-in to a $500 event. I myself bet far too much money on sports at one time in my life. I'll try to show you how to avoid this and other mistakes.

Stick with Poker

Unless you're an expert, don't gamble on anything other than poker. I've just given you an entire book of material on championship poker play, and even reading it won't be enough to make you a great player (as I said, you have to put in the work yourself). So what makes people think they can win a bunch of money betting sports, or playing video poker, or making proposition wagers? Even worse, why would anyone play an obviously negative-EV like craps or roulette? Yet I see poker pros playing these games all the time. Poker requires its players to gamble, if they're going to play the game well. That's a fact I've made clear throughout the book. So I guess I can see why the temptation exists for poker players to gamble on other casino games. Resist the temptation. If you have to gamble, play more poker. Don't become a sports bettor without spending at least a year learning the tools of the trade, just as you did with poker.

Be Cautions of New Friends

After you make your big score, you may learn that you have a lot more "friends" than you previously thought. This may sound like common sense, but please don't just give away money to anyone who asks for it. I know, I know, you're saying now that you would never do that. But I've seen people who, once they've fallen into some money, just hand out hundred-dollar bills to any railbird that happened to be rooting for them. In fact, I once heard of a player giving several thousand dollars to a guy who had bubbled, *just because he felt sorry for him.* If this sounds ludicrous to you, it should, but some players just don't know what to do when money falls into their laps. They're so happy, and they want to share that happiness with anyone who has a forlorn look on his face. It's not easy to win money gambling, it just looks like it is. The money you won playing poker—it didn't just fall into your lap. Be smarter than anyone else. Hold on to your money. Think of how hard you worked to get that money. Don't just give it away.

What Happens if You Blow It All?

At the poker table, you've got to be willing to put all your chips into the pot at any time. In real life, you don't ever risk all your assets on anything. I guess if a sure thing existed, you could risk all your assets on it, but we all know about sure things— they're about as common as free lunches. I had to learn the hard way that money has to be respected. I hope you can take my word for it. But if the unthinkable happens, and you blow off all the money you've won in a big tournament, don't despair. You can get a second chance. Before doing anything, think through all the mistakes you made to lose your fortune. Unlike in poker, where you can do everything right and still lose all your chips, you *must* have made a mistake if you used to have a million dollars and now you have none. Once you find your mistake, you have to convince someone else you won't make it again. Notice that I didn't say you have to convince yourself. It's easy to convince yourself. Find someone you love and trust and tell them the whole story of how you blew a million dollars. If you can convince them that if and when you come into money the next time, you won't blow it, then you have my permission to start back on the road to poker greatness. Keep your ego out of it. If you have to play lower limits for a while, then so be it. Those games should help to teach respect for money.

It is my sincere belief that the above paragraph won't apply to 99 percent of my readers. My readers are going to win on the World Poker Tour, and they're going to approach their success with class, brains, and common sense. Maybe you'll invite Matt and me to the house you buy with your winnings. Maybe you'll quit poker and cure cancer. Who knows? Just remember, the money you make at a WPT final table is real. For example, you could probably buy a hundred thousand copies of this book if you win a WPT event (that would actually be a purchase I highly recommend!). The point is, winning money doesn't give you a license to waste money. As poker players, we don't have the luxury of a steady income. So it's important that we not get too excited after a win, or too down after a loss. It's all just part of the long run.

Of course, you can get a little excited when you see yourself on TV, watching Mike Sexton give you that beer toast. And you're allowed to take some pride in your victories. Poker is something I do professionally, and it's something you, the reader, obviously take very seriously. So claim the rewards you can, but do so in a professional manner. Maybe then I'll see you at not one, but many final tables.

Poker as a Sport

Poker has become to the early 21st century what baseball was in the middle of the last century—America's national pastime. It might seem as though there is a lot of poker on television right now, but think back to when baseball first came on the air. Simply watching all seven games of the World Series live was an astounding new way to follow the game. Now there are thousands of televised baseball games every year. In fact, an untelevised major league baseball game is an embarrassment to the franchises involved.

I'm not necessarily saying we'll get to the point where every major final table is televised live, but I think we'll get a lot closer to that than people realize. We may indeed one day look back at the first three seasons of *World Poker Tour* and say, "Wow, we only got to see the hole cards of the final six players?" Poker is just starting to take its place as one of the major American spectator sports, right up there with auto racing, golf, and tennis. *World Poker Tour* is almost solely responsible for poker's meteoric rise.

As a player I've been in the unique position of getting in at the start of competitive poker history. It's very possible that one day players like Howard Lederer and Daniel Negreanu will be spoken of in hushed tones the same way baseball fans speak of Cy Young and Ty Cobb. That's why I think it's so exciting to be competing on the World Poker Tour today, and that's why I want everyone reading this book to get out there and try to become a part of history. I don't just want to be known as a great poker player, I want to be known as someone who understood

One More Time: Play to Win, Not to Survive!

So make me proud. Review what you've learned. I'll even
help—here's the book in one paragraph. *Play to win, not to survive.*
Always be mentally and physically prepared, as well as confident.
Don't give up; use all the weapons at your disposal at all times.
Learn how to play after the flop. Don't be a player who's afraid to
take risks, or a player who wants to wait for a huge hand before
getting involved. Be a player that everyone else at the table is
afraid to tangle with. Don't be complacent when you get close to
the money in a big tournament. Play to win, not to survive. (It
warrants being said again and again!) Take advantage of the players who are afraid to go broke. Always accept that you have to
risk going broke at some point in order to win the tournament.
Don't relax when you get heads-up. Play to win the whole
freakin' thing.

Practice Is the Only Sure Way to Win

One last thing. There's only so much you can learn from a
book. Don't be discouraged if you go out there and whiff 10 or
20 or 100 satellites before you figure this game out. There's a big
difference between knowing what to do and actually doing it.
There's also a big difference between writing about how to rec-
ognize a weak player at the table and actually sitting down and
taking advantage of that weak player in a World Poker Tour
event. The good news is this book will put you way ahead of a lot
of the competition. The rest of the news is that you have a lot of
work to do yourself if you want to reach the highest level.

Erick with his parents after winning the PPT at the Commerce

I'm grateful to Steve Lipscomb and the WPT for making what I do for a living possible and cool! I'm living a life I never dreamed of. I'm respected, feared, and thriving on the WPT tour and am a very lucky and thankful guy.

I started at the lowest limits and became a champion. It takes work, but it's very, very manageable with just a bit of brains and a lot of heart. The way I see it, if some college dropout named Erick Lindgren can win two World Poker Tour events, anyone that puts his or her mind to it can do the same. So I'll see you on Day One, on the bubble, in the money, and, of course, at the final table.

APPENDIX

WORLD POKER TOUR MILLIONAIRES CLUB

The players are listed in the order they joined the club.*

1. Gus Hansen
2. Alan Goehring
3. Hoyt Corkins
4. Paul Phillips
5. Barry Greenstein
6. Antonio Esfandiari
7. Erick Lindgren
8. Martin de Knijff
9. Hasan Habib
10. Eli Elezra
11. Doyle Brunson
12. Lee Watkinson
13. Daniel Negreanu

14. Erick Brenes
15. Carlos Mortensen
16. Tuan Le
17. Humberto Brenes
18. John Stolzmann
19. Michael Mizrachi
20. Danny Nguyen
21. Michael Gracz
22. David Minto
23. Phil Ivey
24. Paul Maxfield

*As of April 27, 2005.

WORLD POKER TOUR ALL-TIME MONEY LEADERS

PLAYER	WINNINGS	WINS	EVENT/PLACE
Tuan Le	$4,405,738.00	winner (x2)	Foxwoods (1st) Championship 3 (1st)
Daniel Negreanu	$4,176,774.00	winner (x2)	PokerStars 2 (3rd) PartyPoker 2 (2nd) Borgata 3 (1st) Bellagio 3 (1st) Tunica 3 (3rd)
Martin De Knijff	$2,728,356.00	winner	Championship 2 (1st)
Hasan Habib	$2,268,598.00		Championship 2 (2nd) Championship 3 (3rd)
Michael Mizrachi	$2,148,150.00	winner	Tunica 3 (5th) Commerce 3 (1st)
Gus Hansen	$2,150,876.00	winner (x3)	Bellagio (1st) Commerce (1st) Bellagio 2 (3rd) Battle (6th) PokerStars 2 (1st) Bad Boys (1st) Bay 101 3 (3rd)
Erick Lindgren	$1,760,257.00	winner (x2)	Paris 2 (5th) Aruba 2 (1st) PartyPoker 2 (1st) Commerce 3 (5th)
Paul Maxfield	$1,698,390.00		Championship 3 (2nd)

Humberto Brenes	$1,598,405.00	Invitational 2 (2nd) Foxwoods 3 (3rd) Bellagio 3 (2nd)
Michael Gracz	$1,525,500.00	winner	Party Poker 3 (1st)
John Stolzmann	$1,511,282.00	winner	Tunica 3 (1st)
Barry Greenstein	$1,473,133.00	winner	Tunica 2 (1st) PartyPoker 2 (5th)
Antonio Esfandiari	$1,451,135.00	winner	Lucky Chances (3rd) Commerce 2 (1st) Invitational 2 (6th)
Paul Phillips	$1,395,530.00	winner	Bike 2 (2nd) Bellagio 2 (1st)
Hoyt Corkins	$1,379,262.00	winner	Foxwoods 2 (1st) PokerStars (2nd)
Doyle Brunson	$1,333,247.00	winner	Championship 1 (4th) Legends 3 (1st)
Phil Ivey	$1,153,796.00		Foxwoods (4th) Tunica (2nd) Championship (3rd) Borgata 3 (6th) Reno 3 (3rd) Championship 3 (6th)
Lee Watkinson	$1,091,413.00		Mirage 3 (2nd), Legends 3 (2nd)

PLAYER	WINNINGS	WINS	EVENT/PLACE
Carlos Mortensen	$1,070,500.00	winner	Borgata (4th) Doyle (1st)
Danny Nguyen	$1,025,000.00	winner	Bay 101 3 (1st)
Eli Elezra	$1,024,574.00	winner	Mirage 3 (1st)
Alan Goehring	$1,011,886.00	winner	Championship (1st)
David Minto	$1,000,000.00		PartyPoker 3 (2nd)
Erick Brenes	$1,000,000.00	winner	Aruba 3 (1st)
Temp Hutter	$973,256.00		Foxwoods (2nd)
Haralabos Voulgaris	$904,122.00		Commerce 3 (2nd)
John Gale	$890,600.00	winner	PokerStars (1st)
Surinder Sunar	$849,825.00	winner	Paris (1st)
Chau Giang	$807,369.00		Tunica 3 (2nd) Invitational 3 (5th)

Layne Flack	$786,900.00	winner	Foxwoods (2nd) Invitational (1st) Aruba 3 (2nd)
Vinny Vinh	$718,485.00		Commerce 2 (2nd)
Matt Matros	$706,903.00		Championship 2 (3rd)
Matthew Cherackel	$700,000.00		PartyPoker 3 (3rd)
Mel Judah	$681,217.00	winner	Bike 2 (1st) Bellagio 2 (6th)
John Juanda	$672,252.00		Bellagio (2nd) Invitational 2 (3rd) Mirage 3 (4th), Aruba 3 (5th), Doyle 3 (6th)
Arnold Spee	$663,380.00	winner	Reno 3 (1st)
Randy Jensen	$656,460.00		Tunica 2 (2nd)
Scotty Nguyen	$635,325.00		Bellagio 1 (6th) Aruba 1 (3rd★) PartyPoker 2 (6th) Mirage 3 (5th) Tunica 3 (4th)
Michael Kinny	$629,469.00	winner	Reno 2 (1st)

PLAYER	WINNINGS	WINS	EVENT/PLACE
Howard Lederer	$614,250.00	winner (x2)	Foxwoods (1st) PartyPoker (1st) Battle (3rd)
David Pham	$612,094.00		Commerce (4th) Doyle (3rd) Foxwoods
Phil Gordon	$610,000.00	winner	Aruba (1★★) Bay 101 2 (1st)
Jay Martens	$600,000.00		Bay 101 3 (2nd)
Devilfish Ulliott	$589,990.00	winner	Tunica (1st)
David Williams	$573,800.00		Borgata 3 (2nd)
Dewey Tomko	$567,503.00		Costa Rica (4th) Bellagio 2 (2nd)
Hung La	$564,312.00		Doyle Brunson (5th) Commerce 3 (3rd)
Mohammed Ibrahams	$563,400.00		Foxwoods 2 (2nd)
David Benyamine	$560,985.00	winner	Paris 2 (1st) Commerce (6th)
Christer Johansson	$539,950.00	winner	Paris (1st)

John Phan	$518,920.00	Championship 3 (4th)
Kirill Gerasimov	$506,625.00	Championship (2nd)
Adam Csallany	$500,000.00	PartyPoker 3 (4th)
Kido Pham	$496,400.00	Doyle Brunson (2nd)
Alex Balandin	$484,700.00	PokerStars (2nd)
Bradley Berman	$470,452.00	Foxwoods3 (4th)
Noli Francisco	$470,000.00	Borgata 2 (1st) winner
Vinne Landrum	$462,851.00	Bellagio 3 (3rd)
Richard Grijalva	$457,408.00	Championship 2 (4th)
Paul Darden	$446,000.00	Lucky Chances (1st) PartyPoker 3 (5th) winner
Tony G	$442,192.00	Paris (5th) Paris 3 (2nd)
Chris Hinchcliffe	$441,463.00	PartyPoker 2 (3rd)

PLAYER	WINNINGS	WINS	EVENT/PLACE
Ted Forrest	$383,477.00		Championship 1 (5th) Commerce 3 (4th)
Rob Hollink	$377,420.00		Championship 3 (5th)
Mike Keohan	$359,245.00		Commerce 2 (3rd)
J.C. Tran	$353,850.00		Foxwoods (5th)
Ron Rose	$337,798.00	winner	Foxwoods (6th) Reno (1st) Battle (1st)
James Tippin	$328,230.00		Tunica 2 (3rd)
Blair Rodman	$327,815.00		Reno 3 (2nd)
Phil Hellmuth, Jr.	$325,700.00		Lucky Chances (4th) Aruba (4th ★) Foxwoods 2 (3rd)
Russell Rosenblum	$322,660.00		Championship 2 (5th)
Paul 'Eskimo' Clark	$310,403.00		Reno 2 (2nd)

Mikael Westerlund	$306,400.00		PokerStars (3rd)
Daniel Larsson	$300,745.00		Aruba 2 (2nd)
Jennifer Harman	$299,492.00		Aruba (2★★) Ladies (6th) Bellagio 3 (4th)
Josh Arieh	$286,900.00		Borgata (3rd)
Shandor Szentkuti	$280,000.00		Bay 101 3 (4th)
Chip Jett	$276,325.00		PartyPoker (2nd) Bike 2 (4th)
Chris Karagulleyan	$273,000.00	winner	Bicycle (1st) Battle (5th)
Pete Lawson	$272,665.00		Bike (3rd)
Steve Zolotow	$259,684.00		PartyPoker 2 (4th)
Gabe Kaplan	$256,519.00		Mirage (3rd)
Jim Overman	$254,950.00		Paris (3rd)
Daniel Rentzer	$253,595.00		Commerce (2nd)

PLAYER	WINNINGS	WINS	EVENT/PLACE
Mike Matusow	$250,000.00		Aruba (3rd)
Raja Kattamuri	$247,630.00		Tunica 3 (6th)
Corey Cheresnick	$240,000.00		Bay 101 3 (5th)
Charlie Shoten	$235,000.00		Borgata (2nd)
Steve Brecher	$232,862.00		Championship 2 (6th)
Andrew Bloch	$227,810.00		Foxwoods (3rd) Commerce (3rd)
Christopher Ackerman	$226,925.00		Foxwoods 2 (4th)
Bill Gazes	$226,890.00		Commerce 2 (4th)
Steve Rassi	$217,812.00		Bellagio 3 (5th)
Men Nguyen	$210,000.00		Invitational 1 (4th) Bay 101 3 (6th)
Patrick Hocking	$207,700.00		PokerStars (4th)

Chip Reese	$207,304.00	Tunica 2 (4th)
Jan Boubli	$201,818.00	Paris 2 (2nd)
Richard Kain	$200,000.00	PartyPoker 3 (6th)
Chris Moneymaker	$200,000.00	Bay 101 2 (2nd)
Anthony Fagan	$194,230.00	Aruba 2 (3rd)
Can Kim Hua	$184,502.00	Bicycle (5th) Tunica 2 (5th)
Chris Tsiprailidis	$181,200.00	Borgata (4th)
Abraham Mosseri	$174,585.00	Bellagio 2 (4th)
Claude Cohen	$172,784.00	Paris (2nd)
Grant Helling	$170,175.00	Bike (4th)
Adam Schoenfeld	$170,170.00	Commerce 2 (5th)
Patrick McMillian	$170,000.00	Aruba (4th)

PLAYER	WINNINGS	WINS	EVENT/PLACE
Peter Roche	$169,963.00		Paris (4th)
T.J. Cloutier	$165,709.00		Reno (6th) Bike 2 (3rd)
Erik Seidel	$165,000.00		Doyle Brunson (4th)
V. Senthil Kumar	$164,325.00		Foxwoods 2 (5th)
Jose Rosenkrantz	$158,730.00	winner	Costa Rica (1st) Battle (2nd)
"Miami" John Cernuto	$155,800.00		PokerStars (5th)
Harry Knopp	$155,202.00		Reno 2 (3rd)
Harley Hall	$154,992.00		Commerce 3 (6th)
Phil Laak	$154,075.00	winner	Bike 2 (6th) Invitational 2 (1st)
Nam Le	$152,468.00		Bellagio 3 (6th)
George Paravoliasakis	$151,420.00		Paris 2 (3rd)

Chris Bigler	$150,604.00	Bellagio (5th) Lucky Chances (2nd)
Johnny Donaldson	$145,065.00	Tunica (3rd)
Kassem Deeb	$139,120.00	Bellagio (3rd)
Brandon Moran	$135,900.00	Borgata (5th)
Michael Benedetto	$132,600.00	PokerStars (4th)
Joe Awada	$132,200.00	Bike (5th)
Tino Lechich	$130,940.00	Bellagio 2 (5th)
Ben Roberts	$127,475.00	Paris (5th)
Hon Le	$122,550.00	Bicycle (2nd)
Tony Hartman	$120,927.00	Tunica 2 (6th)
David Oppenheim	$117,500.00	Borgata (3rd)
Brian Haveson	$117,375.00	Foxwoods 2 (6th)

WORLD POKER TOUR ALL-TIME MONEY LEADERS

PLAYER	WINNINGS	WINS	EVENT/PLACE
Barry Shulman	$112,780.00		Aruba 2 (4)
Nenad Medic	$112,500.00		PokerStars (6th)
Dave Colclough	$106,113.00		Paris (6th)
Cowboy Simpkins	$105,540.00		PartyPoker (3rd)
Vic Fey	$105,000.00		Aruba (6th)
Michael Yoshino	$103,521.00		Reno 3 (4th)
Masoud Shojaei	$103,300.00		Bay 101 2 (3rd)
Alex Brenes	$100,000.00	winner	Invitational 3 (1st)
John D'Agostino	$99,450.00		PokerStars (5th)
Tom Lee	$99,150.00		Bike (6th)
Peter Muller	$98,022.00		Reno 2 (4th)

Cal Dykes	$97,772.00	Reno (2nd)
Juha Helppi	$95,000.00	winner	Aruba (1st) Battle (4th)
Jim Meehan	$94,507.00	Mirage (6th)
James Hoeppner	$93,326.00	Championship (6th)
Buddy Williams	$91,620.00	Tunica (4th)
Jamie Posner	$90,965.00	Paris 2 (4th)
Allen Cunningham	$86,392.00	Paris (3rd)
John Hennigan	$83,472.00	Bellagio (4th)
Scott Wilson	$79,800.00	Bay 101 2 (4th)
Maureen Feduniak	$79,155.00	PartyPoker (4th)
Russell Carlson	$77,641.00	Reno 3 (5th)
Remco Schrijvers	$74,587.00	PokerStars (6th)

PLAYER	WINNINGS	WINS	EVENT/PLACE
Tony Bloom	$73,517.00		Reno 2 (5th)
Fred Bonyadi	$69,525.00		Bike 2 (5th)
Ted Harrington	$68,920.00		Aruba 2 (5)
Jeremy Tinsley	$68,715.00		Tunica (5th)
Susan Kim	$68,400.00		Bay 101 2 (5th)
Stan Goldstein	$61,270.00		Bicycle (4th)
Mark Chapic	$60,387.00		Reno 3 (6th)
Pete Giordano	$57,850.00		Foxwoods (5th)
Young Phan	$57,180.00		Reno 2 (6th)
Tommy Grimes	$53,445.00		Tunica (6th)
Steve Shkolink	$53,390.00		Commerce (5th)

Mickey Seagle	$52,875.00	Borgata (5th)
Tim Lark	$52,770.00	PartyPoker (5th)
Tony Le	$50,490.00	Reno (3rd)
Johan Storakers	$50,000.00	Invitational 3 (2nd)
Bob Stupak	$46,715.00	Commerce (6th)
Jamie Ligator	$45,000.00	Costa Rica (2nd)
Dan Coupal	$43,975.00	PartyPoker (6th)
Rick Casper	$43,860.00	Aruba 2 (6)
Randy Burger	$41,125.00	Borgata (6th)
Lee Salem	$40,341.00	Paris 2 (6th)
Dr. Jerry Buss	$40,000.00	Invitational (2nd)
Mark Seif	$38,700.00	Bicycle (4th)

PLAYER	WINNINGS	WINS	EVENT/PLACE
Jacques Durand	$34,557.00		Paris (4th)
Kathy Liebert	$30,575.00		Bicycle (6th) Aruba (3rd★)
Paul Magriel	$29,452.00		Reno (4th)
Vince Burgio	$26,000.00		Lucky Chances (5th)
Luis Milanes	$25,120.00		Costa Rica (3rd)
Isabelle Mercier	$25,000.00	winner	Ladies Night 2 (1st)
Clonie Gowen	$25,000.00	winner	Ladies Night 1 (1st)
Mark Edwards	$23,140.00		Reno (5th)
Tommy Garza	$21,000.00		Lucky Chances (6th)
David Chui	$20,000.00		Invitational (3rd)

Tom Everet Scott	$20,000.00	Invitational 3 (3rd)
Chris Ferguson	$15,000.00	Invitational 3 (4th)
Alain Hagege	$14,039.00	Paris (6th)
Joe Cassidy	$14,000.00	Invitational 2 (4th)
Jamie Anteneloff	$11,510.00	Costa Rica (5th)
Anssi Tuulivirdi	$10,400.00	Aruba (2*)
Men Nguyen	$10,000.00	Invitational 1 (4th)
Harry Demetriou	$10,000.00	Invitational 2 (5th)
R.A. Head	$9,420.00	Costa Rica (6th)
Tony Ma	$7,000.00	Invitational (5th)
Woody Moore	$6,000.00	Aruba (4th*)

PLAYER	WINNINGS	WINS	EVENT/PLACE
Andy Glazer	$6,000.00		Invitational (6th)
Bruce Buffer	$5,000.00		Invitational 3 (6th)
Evelyn Ng	$ –		Ladies Night (2nd)
Annie Duke	$ –		Ladies Night (3rd)

★amateur division ★★pro division

WORLD POKER TOUR
PLAYER OF THE
YEAR AWARD

The WPT Player of the Year Award is given out to the outstanding player who earns the most points from his or her finish at the final table. Season One was Gus Hansen; Season Two was Erick Lindgren; Season Three was Daniel Negreanu. Hopefully we will see your name on this list someday soon!

LEGEND

Place	WPT Points
1st	1000
2nd	700
3rd	600
4th	500
5th	400
6th	300
7th	200

PLAYER	EVENT	PLACE	POINTS
Season 1			
Gus Hansen	Bellagio/Commerce	1st/1st	2000 pts.
Howard Lederer	Foxwoods/PartyPoker	1st/1st	2000 pts.
Phil Ivey	Foxwoods/Tunical/Championship	4th/2nd/3rd	1800 pts.
Layne Flack	Foxwoods/Invitational	2nd/1st	1700 pts.
Ron Rose	Foxwoods/Reno	6th/1st	1300 pts.
Andrew Bloch	Foxwoods/Commerce	3rd/3rd	1200 pts.
Chris Bigler	Bellagio/Lucky Chances	5th/2nd	1100 pts.
Alan Goehring	Championship	1st	1000 pts.
David "Devilfish" Ulliott	Tunica	1st	1000 pts.
Christer Johansson	Paris	1st	1000 pts.

Season 2

Erick Lindgren	Paris/Aruba/PartyPoker	5th/1st/1st	2400 pts.
Hoyt Corkins	Foxwoods/PokerStars	1st/2nd	1700 pts.
Paul Phillips	Bike/Bellagio	2nd/1st	1700 pts.
Gus Hansen	Bellagio/PokerStars	3rd/1st	1600 pts.
Daniel Negreanu	Paris/PokerStars/PartyPoker	7th/3rd/2nd	1500 pts.
Barry Greenstein	Tunica/PartyPoker	1st/5th	1400 pts.
David Benyamine	Paris/Commerce	1st/6th	1300 pts.
Antonio Esfandiari	Commerce/Invitational	1st/6th	1300 pts.
Mel Judah	Bike/Bellagio	1st/6th	1300 pts.
Phil Laak	Bike/Invitational	6th/1st	1300 pts.

PLAYER	EVENT	PLACE	POINTS
Season 3			
Daniel Negreanu	Borgata/Bellagio/Tunica	1st/1st/3rd	2600 pts.
Tuan Le	Foxwoods/Championship	1st/1st	2000 pts.
David Pham	Doyle Brunson/Foxwoods	3rd/6th	1400 pts.
Lee Watkinson	Mirage/Bike	2nd/2nd	1400 pts.
Michael Mizrachi	Tunica/Commerce	5th/1st	1400 pts.
Humberto Brenes	Foxwoods/Bellagio	3rd/2nd	1300 pts.
John Juanda	Mirage/Aruba/Doyle Brunson	4th/5th/6th	1200 pts.
Chau Giang	Tunica/Invitational	2nd/5th	1100 pts.
Maciek Gracz	PartyPoker	1st	1000 pts.
John Stolzman	Tunica	1st	1000 pts.
Doyle Brunson	Bike	1st	1000 pts.
Danny Nguyen	Bay 101	1st	1000 pts.

POKER MATH

BY MATT MATROS

POKER MATH, PART 1

Everyone is afraid of math. Teenagers hate algebra, checkout clerks shut down without a calculator, politicians hire teams of "experts" to crunch their numbers, and poker players don't want to hear about odds and equity—or at least a lot of them don't. The very idea that mathematics is useful in poker brings out righteous indignation from a substantial number of today's playing population.

I'm not afraid of math, and I'm going to use the pages of this book to show that nobody else should be afraid of math, either. I was a mathematics major at Yale University, but I definitely don't use complex analysis, differential equations, or algebraic topology at the poker table. Trust me, most of the math that's used in poker can be understood by anyone with a high school education. There are people out there pursuing advanced game theory studies about poker, but we won't get into those. My purpose is to teach the average player everything he needs to know to be wholly math-literate at the table. Let's start by looking at some of the most basic terms used in poker math.

1. Odds

Some gamblers might have heard this word over and over again without really knowing what it meant. Odds are a cousin of probability. So, what's probability? Probability is the chance that a given event will take place. When the weatherman says there is a 25 percent chance of rain today, he is expressing a probability. He is saying the probability that it will rain today is 25 percent. What that means is that if today happened 100 times, 25 of those times it would rain, and 75 times it wouldn't. This brings us back to odds. Odds compare the number of times an event will happen to the number of times it won't. In our weatherman example, the odds against rain falling today would be 75 to 25—that is, for every 75 times that it wouldn't rain, it would rain 25 times. We write these odds as 75 to 25. It is equivalent to express these odds as 3 to 1, because we can see that for every time it rains, it doesn't rain three times (75 divided by 25 equals 3).

Let's look at the probabilities and the odds for some different events.

Coin flip, heads: probability 50 percent, odds 1 to 1

Airline flight delayed: probability 12.5 percent (data from Bureau of Transportation Statistics), odds 7 to 1

Picking the ace of spades out of a deck: Probability 1/52 = 1.9 percent, odds 51 to 1 (in this case, it's easier to do the odds)

In a game like Texas Hold 'Em, we are interested in questions like "What are the odds against completing a four-card flush draw after the flop?" This is a much harder question than "What are the odds against completing a four-card flush draw after the turn?" In the latter case, there is only 1 card left to come. There are 46 unknown cards at that point (52 minus the 2 in our hand and the 4 on the board). So, to calculate our odds of making a flush draw after the turn, we just compare the number of unknown cards that don't help us (37) to the number of unknown cards that do (9). The odds of making a flush draw after the turn, therefore, are 37 to 9, or about 4.1 to 1.

After the flop, with two cards still to come, it's not as straightforward. If we don't make our flush on the turn, we could still make it on the river. How do we account for this? We do it by counting the different combinations of cards that could come. Say we hold the 9♥-8♥ and the flop is 10♥-4♥-2♣. The turn and river could be A♥-K♠. They could be A♥-A♠. They could be 3♥-3♠. They could be J♣-J♦. Each of these is a different combination of turn and river cards. Note that J♣-J♦ is the same combination as J♦-J♣, because they result in the same board. Now, instead of counting cards to determine our odds, we count combinations. If you write down every last possible combination for the turn and river in this hand, it turns out that there are 1,081. Then, if you look closely at all of them, it turns out that 378 result in a flush for our hand. So, the odds against making a four-card flush draw after the flop are 703 to 378 (because 1,081 minus 378 is 703), or about 1.86 to 1.

Just by learning these two terms, you now know how to calculate the odds against making any Hold 'Em hand after the flop, or after the turn. Cool, huh? It is cool, but it's also a lot of work to calculate your odds for every draw you might run into. Luckily, you don't have to, as I'll explain.

3. Outs

Your outs are the number of cards in the deck that will improve your hand. The flush draw we held above had nine outs. An open-end straight draw has eight outs. Two overcards have six outs. You could go through the odds calculation for each of these draws—or you could just read the results off the chart.

NUMBER OF OUTS	TURN AND RIVER COMBINATIONS THAT DO NOT IMPROVE YOUR HAND	TURN AND RIVER COMBINATIONS THAT DO IMPROVE YOUR HAND	ODDS AGAINST IMPROVING (to the nearest 10th)
21 (two overcards and an open-end straight flush draw)	325	756	1-2.3
18	406	675	1-1.7
15	496	585	1-1.2
14	528	553	1-1.0
13	561	520	1.1-1
12	595	486	1.2-1
10	666	415	1.6-1
9	703	378	1.9-1
8	741	340	2.2-1
6	820	261	3.1-1
5	861	220	3.9-1
4	903	178	5.1-1

Notice that with 14 outs or more, we're actually more likely than not to improve.

POKER MATH, PART 2

Poker math isn't for just the nerd faction of poker players, it's for everyone. If you can add, subtract, multiply, and divide, you can use mathematics as a weapon at the table. In the last section, I explained the everyday poker math terms "odds," "combinations," and "outs."

Now we want to take on "range of hands," "pot odds," and "equity," and show why they are important. I often hear this advice: "Don't put your opponent on a specific hand, but on a range of hands." It's good advice, but it's not quite enough. Let's explore this advice from a mathematical standpoint, using a hypothetical (but realistic) poker situation. You have raised with a medium pair—say, 8-8—in No Limit Hold 'Em, and an opponent has reraised you all in. You "know" your opponent has either A-K or a big pair—queens or better. By "knowing" this, you have assigned your opponent a range of hands. That's great, but now what do you do? You're either a big underdog (4.5 to 1 if your opponent has an overpair) or a small favorite (about 1.2 to 1 against A-K). But that doesn't necessarily mean you should fold. You have to go a few steps further.

First, you have to determine the number of hands against which you're a small favorite or a big underdog. But, Matt, you might say, I'm a big underdog against three hands—queens, kings, and aces—and a small favorite against one hand—A-K. Right? No. This is where combinations come in.

In Hold 'Em, there are six preflop combinations that give you pocket aces. You can't get aces any other way. In fact, there are six ways you can be dealt any specific pocket pair. There are, however, 16 ways you can be dealt any specific unpaired hand. Take A-K. You can have any of the four aces with any of the four kings. Four times four is 16. So, in the example above, there are 18 ways (six combinations for queens, six for kings, and six for aces) your opponent can have an overpair, and 16 ways he can have A-K.

OK, now you've counted correctly, and it is more likely, by a score of 18 to 16, that you are against an overpair than A-K. You're a big underdog to an overpair, and only a small favorite against A-K. Now you can fold, right? Wrong. We are missing a vitally important piece of information—namely, the size of the pot. If your opponent's raise is small enough, you should call all-in even though you're likely to be a big underdog. I'll explain why.

In poker, we are often comparing the amount of money we have to call to the amount of money in the pot. The ratio of these two amounts is our pot odds. For example, with blinds of $1-$2, I raise to $6, and my opponent moves all-in for $21. Everyone else folds. I have to call $15 ($21 − $6) to win $30 ($21 + $6 + $2 + $1). My pot odds are 30 to 15, which is equivalent to 2 to 1. So how often do we need to win the pot in order to call when our pot odds are 2 to 1? Well, every time we win, we triple our $15 investment ($15 + $30 = $45). So, if we lose twice in a row but win the third time, we break even. Therefore, we need to win more often than one time in three to make calling correct; we have to be a 2-to-1 underdog or less.

Here's another way to look at it: If you are a 2-to-1 underdog to win the pot, that means one time in three, or about 33 percent of the time, you will win the pot. In this situation, we poker math types like to say that you have 33 percent equity. If there is $30 in the pot and we have to call $15, we will break even if we have 33 percent equity. To prove this, let's say we call. The pot becomes

$45. We are worth 33 percent of that $45, which equals $15. This is the same amount of money that we had to call in the first place. Let's say the pot had been $31 and we had to call only $14, still with the same 33 percent equity. Now if we call, the pot still becomes $45, and we are still worth $15. That's a dollar more than it cost us to call, so in the long run, we make $1 by calling. We make money because our pot odds were 31 to 14. We needed only 31 percent equity (14 divided by 45) to make calling correct, and we had 33 percent. If you compare your equity with the equity you need to call based on the pot odds, you can always determine whether to call an all-in raise.

Equity becomes especially useful when thinking about an opponent's range of hands. Let's get back to the pocket eights. If we convert our odds to percentages (something we covered in the previous section), our equity against an overpair is about 19 percent, while our equity against A-K is about 54 percent. That's great, but what's even better is that we can calculate our equity against the range of hands: Q-Q, K-K, A-A, A-K. We determined above that there are 18 ways our opponent can have an overpair, and 16 ways he can have A-K. To get our overall equity, we just weight the different equities and add them. There are 34 combinations of hands our opponent can have (16 + 18 = 34). So, in this case, 18 times 19 percent for the overpairs, plus 16 times 54 percent for the A-K, divided by 34, gives us an overall equity of about 35 percent. (The exact number is 35.8 percent. I got that by using PokerStove, available for free at www.pokerstove.com.)

Our pocket eights will win the hand more than one time in three even if our opponent can have only queens, kings, aces, or A-K. So, if we're getting 2-to-1 pot odds, whereby we need only 33 percent equity, we are supposed to call. In fact, if we're getting more than 1.8-to-1 pot odds, we're supposed to call. Many No Limit Hold 'Em players would fold two eights when facing an all-in reraise, even if they were getting 2 to 1 on their money. They are costing themselves chips.

It's very rare that an opponent's range is strong enough to make folding correct when you're getting 2-to-1 pot odds against an all-in. Just look at this example. Our opponent's range was incredibly strong, and it was still correct to call with a measly pair of eights. In real life, few opponents have ranges as strong as the one described here. In addition, once you start calling some all-in reraises, your opponents will be much less likely to come over the top of you in future hands. Always think in terms of your equity, in terms of the value in putting chips into the pot. Don't just say, "I'm either way behind or slightly ahead, therefore I fold."

FOLD EQUITY

Why Aggressiveness Makes Mathematical Sense: A Mathematical Look at Playing A-K in No Limit Hold 'Em

People misuse aggressiveness. They hear the advice "Play aggressive poker" and translate it to "Bluff a lot." Aggressiveness is a lot more than bluffing. Too many players are aggressive by putting in a lot of money with their weak or mediocre hands, but slow-playing their other hands. They even get passive with big hands like A-K, wanting to "look at a flop." This approach is often a recipe for disaster. In this section, I'm going to explain why I think A-K is usually a reraising hand in No Limit Hold 'Em.

Let's say the under-the-gun (UTG) player has raised to three times the big blind at a nine-handed No Limit Hold 'Em table. Three players fold and you look down at A-K offsuit. You have

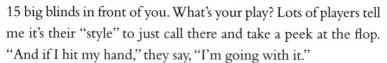

15 big blinds in front of you. What's your play? Lots of players tell me it's their "style" to just call there and take a peek at the flop. "And if I hit my hand," they say, "I'm going with it."

Here is some quick math to show why I think this is bad strategy. First, note that A-K offsuit will miss the flop about two-thirds of the time. So, presumably, we're mucking to a bet on the flop almost two-thirds of the time. I'll allow for some bluff-raises with gut-shot draws from us or for the occasional check-fold from the UTG player, and say that we will have to muck on the flop about 60 percent of the time. Next, let's assign the UTG player a typical UTG range of hands—pocket pairs of sevens or higher, A-Q, A-K, A-J suited.

If we hit the flop with our A-K, pocket pairs of 7-7 through Q-Q hate the flop (unless they flopped a set). They'll bet out a lot of the time—say, 75 percent of the time, anyway—trying to represent top pair, but they'll almost always stop putting money in the pot after we give them action.

So, let's do the math. When we cold-call with our A-K pre-flop, 60 percent of the time we lose just the three big blinds it cost us to call; 10 percent of the time or so, we hit the flop and our opponent check-folds. We win four and a half big blinds (our opponent's raise, plus the blinds who folded before the flop). The other 30 percent of the time is when our opponent bets and we've hit the flop.

If we look at the range of hands we've given him, and assume that he calls our raise only with a set, an overpair, or top pair, we'll see that on about 8 percent of flops, both of us end up all-in. On those flops, we have 40 percent equity ("equity" is a term I covered in the last section). That's right—if our opponent actually wants to get all-in with us, we're an underdog to win the pot. On 22 percent of flops, he bets out and folds to our raise. Let's say he chooses to bet out four and a half big blinds. In that case, we win nine big blinds on the hand (the four and a half from his bet, the three from his preflop raise, and the one and a half from the blinds that folded preflop). Add up all of the big blinds we win or lose in every possible scenario, and you'll find out that cold-calling with A-K against that UTG player's raise wins about 0.4 big blinds per hand in the long run, which is not bad. But A-K is supposed to be a big hand. We're not supposed to be satisfied with winning less than a small blind with it.

Now let's compare flat-calling to the play I recommend— moving all-in preflop. If we move in (jam), I'm going to assume that the UTG player mucks his sevens, eights, nines, A-J suited, and A-Q offsuit, but calls us with A-Q suited, A-K, and pairs of tens or higher. If we look at the money we win when he folds, compared to the money we lose when he calls, it turns out that in the long run, we earn 1.2 big blinds per hand by jamming with A-K—triple what we earned by calling. The biggest reason it works out this way is that we got the UTG player to fold a whopping 45 percent of the time preflop when we moved in. If you don't believe that, what hands do you think he calls with that I have him folding? A-Q, nines, and eights? If he calls with all of those hands, jamming is still almost twice as good as calling. By moving all-in, we give ourselves something called fold equity. We have two kinds of equity: our equity in the pot against our opponent's range of hands in a showdown, and our equity in picking up money for free by getting our opponent to fold before the showdown.

Let's go inside the numbers from the above calculations a bit. When we moved in preflop, the UTG player folded 45 percent of the time, and we won four and a half big blinds. The other 55 percent of the time, we lost a little—about one and a half big blinds. As you can see, this was easily offset by the times we picked up the four and a half big blinds without a fight. Also notice that when our opponent had 10s, jacks, or queens, we won the hand about 43 percent of the time. If we had just called, we would've won the hand less than 30 percent of the time. This is because A-K wants to see all five cards. A-K offsuit has a 43 percent shot to beat two queens by the river, but only a 31 percent chance to be beating two queens after the flop. We need to give ourselves a chance to spike an ace on the turn or the river—and if we hit an ace at any point, we want to get paid. We won't get paid if our opponent has an underpair on an ace-high flop and we still have money in front of us. That's why it's important to get the money in before the flop.

You could nitpick the argument I just made. You might say, for example, that I ignored the rest of the players in the hand. But I would say that we want all of those players to fold, and the best way to get them out is to move all-in. You also might say that some players will open from UTG with A-5 offsuit and play badly enough to lose all of their chips on an ace-high flop, or even a king-high flop. I would say that if the player is that bad, you're probably way ahead of him preflop and want to isolate right then and there.

Here is the central point: with hands that want to reach a showdown, like A-K preflop, or a straight flush draw with two cards to come, it's important to get money into the pot as soon as possible. The more money there is in the pot, the harder it is to fold, and the more likely you are to get your showdown. So, don't be one of those passive A-K players. Learn to love the words "I'm all-in."

Inducing the Bluff

by Matt Matros

Giving a Free Card

Many poker players are mortified about giving their opponents free cards. So often, I'll hear a player who lost a hand say something like "I played it wrong—if I had bet the turn he would've folded, and I would've won the pot."

There are many truisms in poker. Here are two: winning the pot is not the most important thing—winning the most money is; and just because you lost a hand, that doesn't necessarily mean you played it badly.

Let's say you're playing No Limit Hold 'Em, and you have a strong, but beatable hand on the turn. Your opponent is a loose, tricky player who is capable of holding just about anything. In this hand, based on the play of the prior streets, you think he might be on a draw. This opponent is smart enough to know he can't call a large bet with just a draw. His play, however, was also consistent with his having the nuts. So he either has a draw or the nuts. He has already checked. There is $200 in the pot, and you each have $150 in front of you.

Now, here's the problem. If you bet your stack, your opponent will only call if he has you beat. But if you check behind your opponent, you are confident he will bet his stack on the river no matter what comes. Your check, however, gives your opponent a free shot to draw out on you, if he is in fact on a draw. Let's assume you don't know what kind of draw he's on, and that if you check behind your opponent you are going to pay off his river bet no matter what. Let's further assume that if your opponent has the nuts right now, you are drawing dead. What is your best play?

First, we'll calculate the equity from betting our stack on the turn. The fraction of the time our opponent is drawing (call it D), we win the pot, $200. The fraction of the time our opponent has the nuts (1-D), we lose our bet, $150. So our equity is $200D - 150(1-D) = 350D - 150$.

So it is profitable to bet the turn when $350D - 150 > 0$, or $D > 150/350 = \sim 42.9$ percent. That is, we make money by betting the turn if there is a greater than 42.9 percent chance our opponent is on a draw. That *doesn't* mean betting the turn is our best strategy in that case, just that it's a profitable strategy.

Next, we'll calculate the equity from checking behind on the turn to call on the river. Let's assume that if our opponent is drawing, he'll hit his draw one-fifth of the time (this would be roughly his chances of hitting a flush draw). When he's drawing, we lose $150 one-fifth of the time (when he hits) and we win

$350 (the pot plus his river bet) four-fifths of the time (when he misses). We also lose $150 when he has the nuts. So our equity is $350(0.8D) - 150(0.2D) - 150(1\text{-}D) = 400D - 150$.

This strategy will be profitable when $400D - 150 > 0$, or $D > 37.5$ percent.

So our opponent needs to be drawing only 37.5 percent of the time for checking behind to earn us money, as compared to 42.9 percent of the time for betting the turn to earn us money. Wait, it gets better.

Let's compare the two equity calculations:

Betting the turn: $350D - 150$

Checking behind: $400D - 150$

Notice that checking behind earns more money *no matter what D is*! However often our opponent has the nuts (unless he always has the nuts, in which case we lose the same $150 every time), betting the turn will be an inferior strategy to giving the free card. This is, of course, because we have an opponent who is committed to bluffing the river no matter what. Against such an opponent, it should actually be obvious that checking behind on the turn to induce the bluff is always better than betting. Calling his bluff is the only way we make money when we're ahead, and we lose the same amount when we're behind. Obviously, if our opponent has the nuts too often, the best strategy is to check behind on the turn with the intention of folding on the river. But if our read is even remotely accurate, and there is more than a 37.5 percent chance that our opponent is on a draw, then inducing the bluff is best. Betting on the turn is never best.

Inducing the bluff is an even better play if you have a good guess at what kind of draw your opponent is on, and you can safely muck the river to a scare card. In that ideal scenario, inducing the bluff wins the maximum when you're ahead, and loses the minimum when your opponent hits his draw.

How many times have you played No Limit or Pot Limit Hold 'Em against a player who can't resist bluffing the river? A player who, if you check behind him on an earlier street, will shove all-in on the next street virtually every time? Let him do it. You'll be a richer poker player for it.

Inducing the Bluff, Redux

We PokerStars players who were lucky enough to spend a week on Paradise Island in the Bahamas witnessed a striking phenomenon there—a loungeful of people playing online poker over the Atlantis's WiFi connection. "Have you ever got the message 'You are not allowed to play on this table'?" one guy asked. No, buddy, but I know what it means. It means some other clown in this room is already playing the game you want to play. I wasn't in the lounge for the big Sunday tournaments, but I can only imagine the temptations of collusion that abounded.

My favorite moment came when my buddy Chris decided to play a late-night Sit and Go on PartyPoker, with a whole bunch of veteran players standing around watching him and giving commentary. Chris won it, of course, but I bring it up because there was one hand I found particularly interesting that I wanted to look at a little more closely.

I don't remember the exact numbers, so I'll fudge them a little. Three players left. Chris has about $2,800 on the button, and the small blind has about $2,400. Blinds are $100-$200. Chris opens for $600 with A♣-8♣. The small blind (a loose, bad player) calls. The big blind mucks. The flop comes A♦-K♥-Q♦. The small blind, who has shown a propensity for making lots of small bets, leads out for $300. What's your play?

I want to first answer the question "What play earns me the most chips in the long run?" Usually, that's the only question we need to answer, but in this case the payout structure is something we absolutely need to consider. But I'm going to ignore it for a second.

OK, first let's assign a range of hands to our opponent. I think he'd make that bet with any flush draw, any pair on the board, some gut shots, and sometimes with absolutely nothing. So I'll give him any suited one-pair ace (30 combinations), and offsuit one-pair aces down to A-5o (84 combos). KQ-K8 (57), QJ-Q9 (36), J-10 (16), 10-9s (4), 10-8s (4), K-x of diamonds (6), J♦-9♦ or J♦-7♦ (3), 10♦-7♦ (1), 9♦-8♦ or 9♦-6♦ (3), 8♦-7♦ or 8♦-5♦ (3), 7♦-6♦ or 7♦-5♦ (2), 6♦-5♦ or 6♦-4♦ (2), and some complete "bluffing" hands like 4-4 or 7-7 (24).

Now, if we call this opponent's bet, I believe he will bet the same $300 with his entire range, except maybe he'll drop some of the stone bluffs. And if we call him again, I think the same $300 bet is coming on the river with a similar range he bet the turn with.

If we move all-in on the flop, I think he'll call with any ace, K-Q, K-J, K-10, Q-J, Q-10, J-10, K-x of diamonds, J♦-9♦ or J♦-7♦, 10♦-9♦ or 10♦-7♦, and, say, half of his remaining flush draws.

OK, calculating the equity from moving in is easier, so let's do that first. Of his 275 possible hand combinations, he folds 71 of them, and calls with the other 204. The pot after our opponent's bet is $1,700, and there will be $5,000 total in the pot if we move in and our opponent calls. Our equity against the range of hands our opponent calls with is 46.9 percent, and it costs us $1,800 to move our opponent in. So our equity is:

$$(71/275){\star}T1700 + (204/275){\star}(.469{\star}T5000 - T1800)$$
$$= T439 + (204/275){\star}T545 = T843$$

Not bad. Now what happens if we call down. Let's assume we call down on any board. The bets will be small, and our opponent is more than capable of bluffing, so I think this assumption is reasonable even if the board brings a four flush or a four straight. Let's say our opponent will bet his entire range minus 44 on the turn, and then he'll lose the 55 on the river but still bet everything else. And he'll bet T300 every time. So what's our equity?

Well, 263/275 of the time, we'll win as often as we win against his whole range minus 44 and 55. (Yes, this ignores the times he turns a set of fours, or turns or rivers a set of fives. But this doesn't matter much, because the idea is just that he'll be bluffing with slightly less frequency. I'm mostly using the pairs as placeholders for that idea.) Against that range, our equity is 55.8 percent. So our overall equity for calling down is:

$$(263/275)^\star(.558^\star T3200 - T900) + (6/275)^\star(T1700) + (6/275)^\star(T2000) = (263/275)^\star(T885.6) + (6/275)^\star (T1700) + (6/275)^\star(T2000) = T928$$

So letting our opponent continue to bet earns us more chips (assuming I am right about how our opponent will play this hand). Indeed, while watching this pot go down, my suggested course of action was to call. But Chris moved in. He justified that there were too many draws, and he couldn't risk free cards that would lower his chip count. Thinking about it myself, I also thought it might be too important to avoid busting out in third place.

This brings us back to the pay structure issue. Sit and Gos are known for their flat pay structure, with third place out of 10 earning 20 percent of the prize pool. The funny thing is, when they get three-handed, the prize structure is three for first, and one for second. This is pretty similar to a typical tournament's three-handed prize structure, and if anything is on the steep side.

Now that we "know" the chip equities for our two plays here, let's see if we can do the tournament equities.

If we move in, we double up our opponent 0.531*(204/275) = 39.4 percent of the time. When that happens, we are left with 5 percent of the chips, and I estimate our tournament equity is about 0.2 (where the prizes are three units for first, and one for second). Our opponent folds 71/275 = 25.8 percent of the time, and we have T3,900. I estimate our tournament equity in that spot to be 1.8. And 0.469*(204/275) = 34.8 percent of the time we are heads-up with (T5,200/T,8000) = 65 percent of the chips.

So our tournament equity for moving in is:
0.394(.2) + 0.258(1.8) + 0.348(0.65*3 + 0.35*1) = **1.34 units**

If we call down, we lose the pot (263/275)*44.2 percent = 42.3 percent of the time, and we're left with (T1,300/T8,000) = 16.3 percent of the chips. I estimate our tournament equity in that position to be about 0.65. We win the pot (12/275) + (263/275)*55.8 percent = 57.7 percent of the time, and we have a weighted average of close to T4,500 chips in those cases. Our tournament equity in that position is about 2.

So our tournament equity for calling down is:
0.423(.65) + 0.577(2) = **1.43 units**

What happened? Well, we win the pot almost as often when we move in (60.6 percent of the time) as when we call down (57.7 percent of the time). This is because our opponent hardly folds any of the hands that end up beating us in the end. Also, sliding into second isn't that important at this stage of the game. First is now worth three times as much as second is.

And now, just to make things really fun, what if this had been four-handed? At that stage, we have the Sit and Go flat structure of 5-3-2. Now sliding up a place really matters. Just take my word for these numbers.

Tournament equity moving in:
$$0.394(.75) + 0.258(3.35) + 0.348(4.125) = 2.60$$

Tournament equity calling down:
$$0.423(3.3) + 0.577(3.45) = 3.39$$

Huh? Protecting ourselves against the draw still doesn't help. In fact, it's a worse mistake at this stage than it would've been three-handed! Does that make sense? Well, yes, it does. Our biggest chance of busting comes when we move in, not when we fail to move in. If we call down, our worst-case scenario leaves us with ⅙ of the chips. In the three-handed case, that still only puts us at about a 60 percent chance of finishing third, in my estimation. If we move in and lose, we only have ¹⁄₂₀ of the chips. In that case, I give us close to a 90 percent chance of finishing third. And this is, of course, worse for us in the four-handed case, when sliding up a spot really matters.

Here's what I take from this. First, against habitual bluffers, letting them bluff is the best play even on a scary board, especially if they're going to (probably correctly) call with their draws anyway. Second, don't let the pay structure get in the way too much. The best chip-EV play is still usually the best play. Third, if you're interested in sliding up a spot, make sure you know how to do it (hint: moving in to fight off draws is not necessarily wise). Fourth, this entire analysis was based on how I thought this specific opponent would continue with his hand. We'd have an entirely different analysis if this guy was going to shut down with all but his monsters on the turn, and/or fold most of his draws to an all-in on the flop.

As I said, Chris went on to win the Sit and Go. And, incidentally, his opponent in this hand folded to Chris's all-in. Pretty boring hand, huh? Hard to imagine anyone would spend any more time thinking about it.

ACKNOWLEDGMENTS

First of all, thanks to you for making it to the end of this book. I hope it was as fun to read as it was in the writing. An author is only as good as his audience.

None of this would have been possible without the commitment of many individuals, especially the dedicated team at World Poker Tour. Special thanks go to founders Steve Lipscomb, Lyle Berman, Audrey Kania, and Robyn Moder for having the guts to push WPT to its well-earned glory. Without their efforts, televised poker would still be huddled in the back room instead of standing proud in the spotlight. The game and sport of Texas Hold 'Em owe a great deal to them.

Thanks to my mom and dad for their endless support, and for taking their own gamble that a son's hobby could turn into a career.

A shout out to my friends and cohorts—Josh Arieh, Antonio

Esfandiari, Daniel Negreanu, Evelyn Ng, and David Williams. These guys make the game worth playing. I also owe a debt of gratitude to the WPT players I've had the opportunity to sit down at a final table with . . . they have all been consummate professionals and worthy adversaries. Much thanks to Brian Balsbaugh at Poker Royalty for legitimizing poker pros and providing us with countless opportunities to enjoy and promote the success this game has given all of us.

I've enjoyed all of my experiences with the WPT and am honored to be a small part of the legacy that they've set out to create. I credit them for taking Hold 'Em to the next level. To the thrill of everyone in the business, the face of poker has changed for countless generations to come. Gratitude must be given to members of the WPT staff for helping me to assemble the nuts and bolts of this book—Andrea Green, Melissa Feldman, Elaine Chernov, Jennifer Newell, and resident homeboy Chris Lockey. I would also like to thank Andy Topkins and the crew at Brandgenuity, as well as Matthew Benjamin and the entire HarperCollins team for their efforts in putting the stage on the page.

And last, but certainly not least, my greatest thanks go to my contributor Matt Matros—strategy *does* come through experience, win or lose.

INDEX

Note: Page numbers in *italics* refer to illustrations.

Now test what you've learned against Erick and othe WPT pros with the World Poker Tour™ video game!

Available now for popular home video game consoles

Take a seat at the world's most prestigious poker tournaments with the World Poker Tour™ video game. Put your skills to the test against the world's best as you compete against real WPT™ players including Erick Lindgren, Antonio "the Magician" Esfandiari, Evelyn Ng, Lyle Berman, Michael "the Grinder" Mizrachi, and Phil "Unabomber" Laak, in re life WPT venues. Custom create poker games by setting rules and limits with the innovative poker editor, and take your game online to set up a poker night with your friends. An exclusi presentation system modeled after the popular World Poker Tour broadcast, with insightful commentary by Mike Sexton and Vince Van Patten, turns your living room into a seat at a WPT table. It's time to *Shuffle Up and Deal!*